PROBLEMS AS

possibilities

Problem-Based

Learning for

K–12 Education

L I N D A   T O R P   A N D   S A R A   S A G E

Association for Supervision and Curriculum Development
Alexandria, Virginia USA

Association for Supervision and Curriculum Development
1250 N. Pitt Street • Alexandria, Virginia 22314-1453 USA
Telephone: 1-800-933-2723 or 703-549-9110 • Fax: 703-299-8631
Web site: http://www.ascd.org • E-mail: member@ascd.org

On July 14, 1998, ASCD will move to new headquarters: 1703 N. Beauregard St., Alexandria, VA 22311-1714.
Telephone: 703-578-9600

Gene R. Carter, *Executive Director*
Michelle Terry, *Assistant Executive Director,*
    Program Development
Nancy Modrak, *Director, Publishing*
John O'Neil, *Acquisitions Editor*
Mark Goldberg, *Development Editor*
Julie Houtz, *Managing Editor of Books*
Margaret A. Oosterman, *Associate Editor*
Charles D. Halverson, *Project Assistant*

Gary Bloom, *Director, Editorial, Design, and*
    Production Services
Karen Monaco, *Senior Designer*
Tracey A. Smith, *Production Manager*
Dina Murray, *Production Coordinator*
John Franklin, *Production Coordinator*
Valerie Sprague, *Desktop Publisher*
Sarah Allen Smith, *Indexer*

Printed in the United States of America.

ASCD Stock No. 198010   ASCD member price: $12.95; nonmember price: $15.95

May 1998 member book (p). ASCD Premium, Comprehensive, and Regular members periodically receive ASCD books as part of their membership benefits. No. FY98-7.

Library of Congress Cataloging-in-Publication Data
Torp, Linda, 1946–
        Problems as possibilities : problem-based learning for K-12
education / Linda Torp and Sara Sage.
        p.   cm.
        Includes bibliographical references and index.
        ISBN 0871202972
        1. Problem-based learning. 2. Curriculum planning. I. Sage, Sara,
1961– II. Title.
        LB1027.42 .T67 1998
        371.39—ddc21
                                                                98-8888
                                                                CIP

03 02 01 00 99 98   6 5 4 3 2 1

To Clyde Torp—my husband, mentor, and best friend

To Andy Sage—my son—who enriches my life every day

Problems as Possibilities:
Problem-Based Learning for K–12 Education

SPECIAL ACKNOWLEDGMENT

The ideas developed in this book were catalyzed by the work of the Illinois Mathematics and Science Academy's Center for Problem-Based Learning and the generous support of The Harris Family Foundation.

ACKNOWLEDGMENTS

We would like to express our gratitude to a number of people who contributed to our work on this book and who helped enrich our understanding of problem-based learning. First, we would like to thank The Harris Family Foundation for their generous support of our work at the Illinois Mathematics and Science Academy's Center for Problem-Based Learning. Our acknowledgment also goes to the Illinois Mathematics and Science Academy (IMSA) for ongoing support.

Numerous individuals affiliated with the Illinois Mathematics and Science Academy's Center for Problem-Based Learning have contributed to the conceptual and developmental process of understanding problem-based learning, and we have all learned from each other. We thank them all, particularly the staff of the Center for Problem-Based Learning, IMSA faculty (past and present), and those teachers with whom we have been in partnership in Illinois and other states. We particularly want to acknowledge the assistance of several IMSA colleagues, Bernard Hollister and John Thompson, who read drafts of this manuscript and engaged in dialogue with us. Sina Fritz was invaluable in providing assistance with graphics and manuscript preparation. Our editors at ASCD, Mark Goldberg and Margaret Oosterman, provided us with helpful feedback, which enabled us to express our understandings effectively, and helped facilitate the entire process. Thanks to all of you!

INTRODUCTION

We can't put it together. It is together.

—Whole Earth Catalog 1971

WHETHER THINKING ABOUT THE UNIVERSE, THE AMBIGU-ities of life, or the wonders of learning—educators realize that the whole is so much more than any collection of parts. As they work with learners of all ages, they constantly strive to create experiences that are holistic and connected. Ones that enable students to tackle the complexities facing us as citizens in a global community, as well as in everyday situations. Ones that reveal a need to be open-minded and adaptable. Ones that consider the interrelatedness of systems, both natural and contrived.

We journey through life encountering, grappling with, and resolving problems that present powerful opportunities for learning. Ask people to describe a time in their lives when they really learned something that they remember with understanding today. Most will not recall a formal educational experience. Many will relate struggling with a problem such as dealing with the death of a parent. What needs to be done? Who needs to know? How will they cope with the news? Is there an estate or mounting liabilities? What are the legal issues? These are just a few of the questions begging consideration and a balanced response.

Messy, ill-structured problems like that one capture our attention and draw us into their depths. They focus our investigation and thinking, bringing us closer and closer to comprehension and resolution. These problems present holistic learning experiences. They expose and connect rich content and essential skills. They catalyze critical and creative thinking. And they place us in situations that demand decisions based upon sound criteria, taking into account conflicting interests and incomplete information. This is problem-based learning—where the problem comes first and learning is fueled through the problem's investigation and resolution.

Since 1992, the Center for Problem-Based Learning at the Illinois Mathematics and Science Academy (IMSA) has investigated and applied the principles of problem-based learning (PBL). Our work there has described how problem-based learning is applied in elementary, middle, and high school settings. We have measured the effects of defined aspects of a problem-based approach. And we have shared our experience and learning with hundreds of educators across the country. (See Appendix for more information on IMSA's Center for Problem-Based Learning.)

This book is a natural extension of that work. But how do we represent a dynamic concept like problem-based learning in a way that enables understanding and encourages application? What can we say in print on the static pages of a book that would meet the needs of a diverse group of learners?

In thinking through our problem as authors, we clearly heard the voices of educators with whom we have worked. Their needs were as diverse as their interests. Some were captivated by stories of real classroom experiences. What happened? Why were the students intrigued by the problem? Others wanted to know about problem-based learning. Where did it come from? How does it relate to other ideas about teaching and learning that are part of the educational scene? Many needed to get involved from the inside and design their own problem-based units. Where do they begin? How does the teacher coach the learning process? All would eventually construct meaning, but their pathways differed.

Our book offers opportunities to learn about PBL from multiple perspectives. All readers will find strong connections to their own classroom experience while learning about problem-based learning.

Experiencing PBL

Chapter 1 tells stories through the comments of teachers and students who have experienced PBL. Vignettes from several grade levels and contexts enable readers to see PBL's possibilities.

Learning About PBL

Chapter 2 provides an overview of problem-based learning, and Chapter 3 presents background information. We hope these chapters supply answers for those who need to know, What is it and where does it come from?

Designing and Implementing PBL

Chapters 4, 5, and 6 allow readers to play with an idea and make it their own. These chapters present practical information to enable educators to design and develop PBL curriculum and plan for instruction in a PBL classroom.

Thinking About PBL

Chapter 7 offers answers for those who need to know the "whys" to find their way through an idea. It builds a solid foundation for PBL as a valuable innovation for today's learners and opens the door to the process of becoming a teacher of PBL.

Different pathways through these chapters help serve the needs of different learners:

- If you are intrigued by context and how ideas play themselves out in authentic settings, begin with Chapter 1.
- If you want to know the origins and the grounding of ideas, begin with Chapter 2, 3, or 7.
- And if you must roll up your sleeves and become immersed in the "how" of things, begin with Chapter 4, 5, or 6.

Wherever you begin (see the figure "Overview of *Problems as Possibilities*" on p. 4.), come full circle to experience the possibilities of problem-based learning as a natural integrating focus for relevant curriculum and meaningful student learning.

FIGURE I.1
Overview of *Problems as Possibilities*

Experiencing PBL
◆ Chapter 1: What Does PBL Look Like in Classrooms?
  • Through the eyes of learners
  • Through the eyes of teachers

Thinking About PBL
◆ Chapter 7: Why PBL?
  • What are your questions?
  • What does it take to become a teacher of PBL?

Learning About PBL
◆ Chapter 2: What Is PBL?
  • Background
  • Comparison of PBL to other instructional strategies

◆ Chapter 3: What Are the Foundations of PBL?

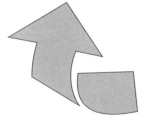

Designing and Implementing PBL
◆ Chapter 4: What Is Our Model for PBL?

◆ Chapter 5: How Do You Design a PBL Curriculum?
  • Teacher as designer
  • Teacher as refiner

◆ Chapter 6: How Do You Implement PBL?
  • Teacher as coach
  • Students as active problem-solvers

1

WHAT DOES PROBLEM-BASED LEARNING LOOK LIKE IN CLASSROOMS?

> To educate is to take seriously both the quest for life's meaning and the meaning of individual lives. . . . Through telling, writing, reading, and listening to life stories—one's own and others'—those engaged in this work [teaching] can penetrate cultural barriers, discover the power of the self and the integrity of the other, and deepen their understanding of their respective histories and possibilities.
>
> —Witherell and Noddings 1991, pp. 3–4

AS WE WORK WITH EDUCATORS FROM AROUND THE COUNtry, we have come to appreciate the power of story. Strong connections are sparked when we relate how teachers organize problem-based learning (PBL) experiences and how students respond. Our partners are enthusiastic and thoughtful PBL practitioners from whom we learn a great deal. We'll begin with their words—their stories.

At Elementary Schools

One important story is being written at Westgate Elementary School in Arlington Heights, Illinois. Educators have been using PBL at least four years, examining how it works best with young students, and adapting the process to a point where their school community— administrators, teachers, students, parents, and business-people—enthusiastically support PBL.

In a recent problem, 1st through 5th grade students investigated difficulties their former principal was having maintaining a healthy flower garden at home. Students examined soil and plant samples from her garden, read about how to grow healthy plants, searched the Internet, contacted local experts, and conducted experiments on growing plants under different conditions.

Several students had difficulty getting adults to take them seriously. Michael, a 4th grader, called a local plant nursery for information about watering plants. The person answering the phone said, "Just don't give them too much water," and then hung up.

Students discussed his dilemma. Andy suggested that Michael should have called back and asked, "How much water is too much?" or kept them on the phone by saying, "Wait a second," or something similar. Eventually the group located an individual who would answer questions to their satisfaction. Students learned something about perseverance and differences among adults.

Teachers at Westgate are excited about how students are learning, and students are excited about learning. Here are their comments:

The way they're doing their experiments and thinking about their experiments before they just rush into doing them—they're reading them over and predicting and deciding whether they're going to be helpful or not—they've definitely surpassed my expectations at this point.

—Linda Zakarian, 1st/2nd Grade Teacher

I saw the kids learn a ton of information about plants, and they know that if they're going to have a garden, they need to really read directions, and they need to know some conditions of sunlight and water. They got out of it what I wanted them to get out of it. They're much more knowledgeable about plants, but I didn't have to do it from a textbook. . . . I've learned to constantly push the kids to keep thinking. If they come up with one answer, don't stop there, because the likelihood is there are at least five more answers.

—Melissa Rabin, 3rd/4th Grade Teacher

[Things have to work together] like the sun and the water. You have to know if it's going to rain or not, and you have to know where to plant your flowers so they get the right amount of sun or shade they need. I think it's weird that sometimes things don't need very much sun but they need a lot of water.

—Richard, 4th Grade Student*

Both students and teachers like the authenticity of PBL, as shown in these comments:

*All student names are fictitious.

I like PBL because it's challenging and fun, because you're learning something new; every problem's a little different 'cause you're going for different goals in the solutions.

—Cal, 4th Grade Student

Some kids question when you're teaching basic skills: "Why do we have to learn this? When are we ever going to do this?" [With PBL] You're showing them a reason, a specific, real-life situation. I'm teaching them basic skills, but I'm giving them a reason.

—Linda Zakarian, 1st/2nd Grade Teacher

Ruth, a student in Zakarian's class, said she liked the plant problem because she could help the former principal solve a real problem. Ruth's mother echoed her daughter's excitement:

Ruth talked a lot about the plant problem; we discussed it a lot. I was impressed with the sources they went to for information, phone calls they made; [they even went] as far as getting an analysis of the soil—that they would *think* about that. Also, I could see on her face that she was very thrilled that she was able to find out information that an adult was very interested in. . . . but also that she just received this level of respect from an adult. It really boosted her confidence. . . . I think problem-based learning empowers children to be real active participants in the world around them when they get the opportunity.

As we interviewed students, we found they identified other skills they had learned during PBL experiences. They described how they helped each other locate and understand information in the plant problem:

[I use a highlighter pen] if there's a picture there with a whole bunch of things, . . . you can highlight [some parts] so you won't need to keep reading it; it tells you what you're reading.

—Jennifer, 1st Grade Student

Some of the people [in my group] looked at pictures and got a little information; then if I read and found something, I would think: Would that make sense? Is it important or not? Sometimes it would be important for *this* but not important for *this*. . . . like all the stuff I read in this book about seeds—I found that animals help scatter seeds; that is important. But the picture was showing a bird taking a cherry, so I wasn't sure [if that was important] because [the principal] might not have any of those kinds of trees.

—Kristen, 2nd Grade Student

Others talked about how they worked in their collaborative small groups while gathering information and determining solutions:

Last year we did a couple of problems, so I've learned last year and this year how to work together and what to do when something is going wrong, like when half of the group wants to go to the learning center and half doesn't; you want to stay here and break down the information. . . . I learned how to compromise with them: "Well, let's split up into two groups."

—Wendy, 2nd Grade Student

> I had all new friends [1st graders] at my table, so I said, "You guys can help me make up some stuff to write down, and we'll put it on a big sheet of paper." I didn't just say, "Okay, I'm going to write this down, I'm going to do this and that," and do all of it.
>
> —Ruth, 2nd Grade Student

Students completed a pre- and post-test in which they were asked to develop instructions on how to grow plants successfully. For her pre-test, Andrea, a 3rd grader, drew four pictures, with little accompanying information (mentioning seeds, sun, and rain). On a post-test in May, however, seven months after completing the plant problem, Andrea wrote instructions that included 10 necessary components for healthy plant growth: soil, seeds, water, fertilizer, sun, rain, carbon dioxide, respiration/breathe, chlorophyll/food, and space to grow (all spelled correctly!). Andrea is a special education student.

Many members of the learning community at Westgate report that they can spot students who have had several experiences with PBL by their behavior. These students are better at dealing with conflicts in the lunchroom or on the playground. They also approach learning differently in the classroom, asking more questions, and refusing to let go of issues until they are satisfied they understand it thoroughly, even to the extent of assigning themselves homework. Another experienced PBL teacher at Westgate, Christine Vitale Ortlund, mentions that now many students don't just ask to learn by solving problems, they actually demand it.

At Middle Schools

An essential part of the middle school story is to find engaging, authentic problems where students are placed in a role and situation that hooks them—at this age they are typically interested in everything *but* academics. One teacher, whose students took the role of village board members examining overdevelopment in Barrington, Illinois, explains how role playing helps students think outside their immediate world:

> If you ask [8th graders] to do something, their first reaction is, "Who cares? I don't care—it doesn't affect me." But if they have a role, then they have to look at it from someone else's perspective and point of view. So they can no longer be a smart aleck 8th grader who doesn't care, but they have to put themselves in some other shoes. So what's fun [the role] for an elementary student becomes even more important as a middle schooler, because it forces them to get into it and to look at [the problem] from a perspective that you'd want them to see it from.
>
> —Maggie Oberg, Language Arts Teacher
> Barrington Middle School, Prairie Campus
> Barrington, Ill.

Several other middle school teachers recognize the importance of students knowing that they own a real problem and that they can really affect their schools or communities:

If you give them [8th grade students] a role of power, then they really buy into this. We've done two problems where kids have been put in the position of making recommendations. . . . about school district policy to school board members, a superintendent, and a principal. And [the students] walked away from that saying, "We could say something. We had something to say and adults listened to us. . . . We may have actually done something for our school—something that's really going to directly affect us."

—Karoline Krynock, Science Teacher
Barrington Middle School, Prairie Campus
Barrington, Ill.

Some students were immediately hooked when they realized they owned the problem. . . . Once they could see that their ideas were indeed valid (or why they were not) according to criteria they provided for themselves, then the grin appeared and momentum picked up.

—Mary Biddle, Social Studies Teacher
Franklin Middle School, Champaign, Ill.

Middle school students can learn a great deal of academic content in well-designed and well-implemented PBL experiences. Karoline Krynock and her PBL teaching partner, Louise Robb, conducted classroom research showing that their PBL students learned as much or more content in a problem designed around the issue of possible genetic causes for aggressive behavior than did students in a more traditional genetics unit (Krynock and Robb 1996). Krynock says that her students learn more "real science" in PBL than in any other teaching method she has used. Robb sees an additional advantage:

Another positive thing is that when you "go public"—we've had some panels of experts come in and hear solutions from our groups—the adults are just astounded by the depth of [students'] knowledge and the kinds of things they've been able to deal with. We've gotten nothing but positive feedback. . . . The kids are asking just incredibly complex questions, which show they do have a lot of understanding of content.

—Louise Robb, Language Arts Teacher
Barrington Middle School, Prairie Campus
Barrington, Ill.

PBL provides many opportunities for students to interact with each other and with content:

The most recent picture of my students working in the library gathering information for a PBL exercise includes different images:

- Students excited about learning.
- Students struggling to learn more about (or understand more in depth) a complicated issue.
- Students who would not normally even talk to each other working together on a topic.
- Students engaging in lively conversations about school work.
- Students sharing magazines and information (not *MAD* but *Scientific American*).

—Nancy Baird, Gifted Resource Teacher
Franklin Middle School, Champaign, Ill.

Lisa Nicholson, a special education teacher at Burr Ridge Middle School in Burr Ridge, Illinois, has found PBL to be an effective strategy with a wide range of students.

With a science teacher, she cotaught two problems for several years—one on deer overpopulation in their area, and one on HIV-positive middle school students. She says that although all students benefit from the real-life problems the teachers have presented in PBL, it is particularly important for special education students, who often don't want to learn or have difficulty learning unless they see a reason behind it. PBL also allows her students to use the learning style that is best for them. And they can demonstrate their knowledge through many different assessment formats, such as oral presentations, debates, and posters.

Other teachers mention that dealing with authentic problems helps students think about ethical aspects of issues they might not have otherwise considered. At the end of a PBL experience dealing with HIV/AIDS, Krynock reported that her class felt strongly that they had an obligation to educate others to reduce fear surrounding the disease. She was surprised and impressed by their maturity and empathy in considering how an HIV-positive student might feel and their subsequent desire to be proactive in providing education with their peers:

> Even if we had read a hundred short stories and memorized a million AIDS pamphlets, I don't know that they would have learned the valuable lessons they learned from the short [time] we spent examining this problem.
>
> —Karoline Krynock, Science Teacher
> Barrington Middle School, Prairie Campus
> Barrington, Ill.

At High Schools

Consider this problem designed as a precursor to reading *To Kill a Mockingbird*:

> Students are members of the Alabama Historical Society, which has been contracted to research a family's background during the time period of the novel *To Kill a Mockingbird*. What was going on in the family during the time period of the novel? How reliable is the information the historical society uncovers? If controversial information about family members arises, who needs to know—or not?
>
> —Yolanda Willis, Language Arts Teacher
> East Aurora High School, Aurora, Ill.

Even though her students normally enjoyed this book, Willis reports that PBL enhanced this American literature unit:

> I think the kids were more *into* what they were doing; it seemed more relevant to them, especially with the social studies teacher [an expert on the 1930s] coming in and talking with them. . . . What really grabbed them . . . was when I brought the guy in who said that the original person the students were researching had lynched *his* grandfather. So then it became more of an ethical problem—the kids had to go back to their problem statement and decide: "Maybe we shouldn't even be doing this." Before that, it was: "Okay, we'll do this; we'll do all the research and make all the pictures." But when [that ethical dimension] came in, they were like: "Wow!" It really blew them away.

Teachers can design PBL problems around interdisciplinary issues as well. Another teacher relates this story of student empowerment:

> There's a metamorphosis that you cannot even begin to contemplate. I listened to one girl who was being interviewed by the [*Chicago Tribune*] on the phone. Crissy said, "I never knew I could do all this; I didn't know I was such a good thinker; I didn't used to be able to get up in front of people and speak. . . ." I love to see the depth of their thinking and hear realizations that they're operating on a different level. . . . I like to see the metamorphosis in staff that are the audience for their exhibitions. Administrators are seeing kids differently. Other teachers are saying, "Yes, kids can do." I've always believed kids can do anything, but it's so exciting to see that happen.
> —Ellen Jo Ljung, Language Arts Teacher
> Glenbard West High School, Glen Ellyn, Ill.

Real-life problems can become PBL problems, as shown in these examples:

- Bernard Hollister, a social science teacher, coteaches a PBL course, Science, Society, and the Future (SSF), for seniors at the Illinois Mathematics and Science Academy (IMSA). SSF students recently started the year with a problem Hollister designed around lunchroom waste in U.S. schools. As he puts it, students began "stripping away the layers of the onion" when they discovered that lunchroom waste was only the tip of this problem. The real problem seemed to be flawed methodology and strong political motivations in the congressional study they were using.

- Also at IMSA, science/physics teacher David Workman has used PBL for a number of years. One of his recent problem units in his Integrated Science course revolved around finding the best possible design for retention/detention ponds in the immediate school vicinity. There had been severe flooding in the community last year. In this course, students investigate "problem platforms," which expose physical and biological problematic contexts—such as pond life or habitation on Mars. Such exposure allows students to be involved in several different PBL experiences.

- John Thompson, an IMSA science/biology teacher, uses PBL in several science classes. For a predator unit in his ecology class, John focuses on the central issue of wolf reintroduction into natural habitats. Each year he updates this core problem to reflect a current real-world scenario.

- A science/chemistry instructor, Richard Dods, has developed a biochemistry course around realistic problem scenarios, such as learning about isoenzymes by diagnosing, as cardiologists, the source of chest pain in the character Miles Silverberg from television's "Murphy Brown."

High school students participating in PBL clearly enjoy the strategy as well as find it beneficial in preparing them for their future:

I like Comm-Tech [Communications Technology course] because it's a class where you take all the material you've learned and you use it. . . . Other classes teach you *what* to learn; this class teaches you *how* to learn. I think I'll actually use this class when I move on into computer science and electrical engineering; it teaches you how to solve problems on the job.

—Don, Student in Ellen Ljung's class
Glenbard West High School, Glen Ellyn, Ill.

[PBL] is a different approach to education. Instead of: "Here's a sheet of vocabulary words, memorize them," you could say, "Well, this happens, you know—why? Now go find out. See what you can find out about the why or the how of something. . . ." There's usually not one right answer. There can be more than one answer, or there isn't one; you form a new question and go from there.

—Cindy, Student in John Thompson's Ecology Class
Illinois Mathematics and Science Academy, Aurora, Ill.

The skills I learned in [John Thompson's] ecology class have been helpful both in terms of the research and studying that I've done for my college courses and also the research that I've done for my own research career. . . . That series of thought processes that takes you from complete ignorance to a knowledge that's focused and can answer a specific question is a very useful thing to know, and it's a very difficult skill to learn, I think, in most school settings.

—Elizabeth Pine, Former IMSA Student
1993 Westinghouse Science Talent Search
Competition Award Winner

* * *

Stories from teachers, students, and parents are powerful. But what is this thing called problem-based learning? What do we know about PBL? What do teachers and students do in PBL? How can you design problems for your class? How can you write your own PBL story? These questions and others are addressed as you investigate PBL in this book.

2

WHAT IS
PROBLEM-BASED LEARNING?

NEARLY EVERY DAY, WE FACE POSSIBILITIES AND PROBLEMS that affect our personal and professional lives. The ability not only to cope but also to identify key issues, access information, and effectively work our way through these situations contributes to success in whatever we pursue. Building a mental network of these experiences enables us to make connections through association and interpretation. This "context-building knowledge gives form to everything we do or think or feel, on the job, in the voting booth, in the home" (Broudy 1982, p. 578).

Most of us are familiar with teaching models in which we first learn identified content and processes through lecture, direct instruction, and guided discovery. Then we apply this new learning in well-structured situations, problem sets, and forced-response items designed to see if we understand or have mastered what was taught. This teaching paradigm, with a teach, learn, and apply sequence, has been the standard in our schools for quite some time. Roles are clear: Teachers teach; students learn. If only it were that simple.

Problem-based learning refocuses our practice to what some call a learning paradigm. PBL confronts students with a messy, ill-structured situation where they assume the role of the stakeholder or "owner" of this situation. They identify the real problem and learn whatever is necessary to arrive at a viable solution through investigation. Teachers use real-world problems and role playing as they coach learning through probing, questioning, and challenging student thinking. Here are some examples:

Second grade students serve as advisors to NASA. A planet much like Earth has experienced massive destruction of the elements in its biosphere. What is causing the destruction of plant life? Can new plants from Earth be successfully introduced to help save the planet's environment? How can we find out?
—Rawls Byrd Elementary School, Virginia

Middle school students act as scientists with the State Department of Nuclear Safety. Some people in a small community feel their health is at risk because a company keeps thorium piled above ground at one of their plants. What are the critical issues? Who else is concerned? What is the extent of our authority? What action, if any, should be taken?
—Summer Challenge Program
Illinois Mathematics and Science Academy, Illinois

High school basic composition students serve as consultants to the warden of a women's correctional facility. They examine the potential causes of recidivism among women prisoners. Why don't these women succeed in society? What communication skills would help the women improve their chances? How can these "consultants" design a program to address prisoner needs?
—East Aurora High School, Illinois

Defining Problem-Based Learning

Problem-based learning is focused, experiential learning (minds-on, hands-on) organized around the investigation and resolution of messy, real-world problems. It is both a *curriculum organizer* and *instructional strategy*, two complementary processes. PBL includes three main characteristics:

- Engages students as stakeholders in a problem situation.
- Organizes curriculum around this holistic problem, enabling student learning in relevant and connected ways.
- Creates a learning environment in which teachers coach student thinking and guide student inquiry, facilitating deeper levels of understanding.

We see a PBL curriculum as providing authentic experiences that foster active learning, support knowledge construction, and naturally integrate school learning and real life, as well as integrating disciplines. The problematic situation is the organizing center for curriculum. It attracts and sustains students' interest with its need for resolution while exposing multiple perspectives. Students are engaged problem solvers, identifying the root problem and the conditions needed for a good solution, pursuing meaning and understanding, and becoming self-directed learners. Teachers are problem-solving colleagues who model interest and enthusiasm for learning *and* are also cognitive coaches who nurture an environment that supports open inquiry (see Figure 2.1 on p. 16).

Overview of PBL Design and Implementation

Designing and implementing a PBL unit are two interrelated processes that balance the needs of students and the curriculum within a particular learning context. Figure 2.2 (see p. 17) shows the main elements in the two processes.

Problem Design

Teachers select possibilities for problem situations by scanning their curriculum and local newspapers, and speaking with community members and colleagues. They think about the characteristics and needs of their learners, looking for ways to hook students:

> The problematic situation has the seeds of interest within it. Students can relate to people attempting to deal with the unknown and living under adverse conditions (Barell 1995, p. 122).

In considering problem possibilities, teachers assess opportunities for "curriculum payback," including integrat-

ing across disciplines and making community connections. This exploration leads to identifying a problem that will enable students to make meaningful connections between school and life while providing educators with powerful curricular connections:

> Problematic situations are robust in that they contain within them significant concepts worth thinking about (Barell 1995, p. 131).

Educators seek out or design scenarios that provide rich opportunities for demonstrating learning through projects, presentations, or other means authentic to the situation. Here is a graphic representation of the PBL process:

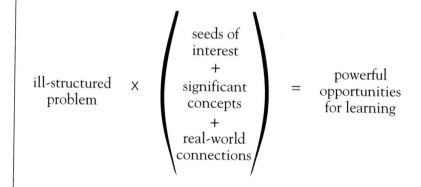

$$\text{ill-structured problem} \times \left(\begin{array}{c} \text{seeds of interest} \\ + \\ \text{significant concepts} \\ + \\ \text{real-world connections} \end{array} \right) = \begin{array}{c} \text{powerful opportunities for learning} \end{array}$$

To develop a PBL unit, teachers decide on a role to frame the students' involvement in a chosen problem. "The learning experience provides students with opportunities to take different perspectives on the subject" (Barell 1995,

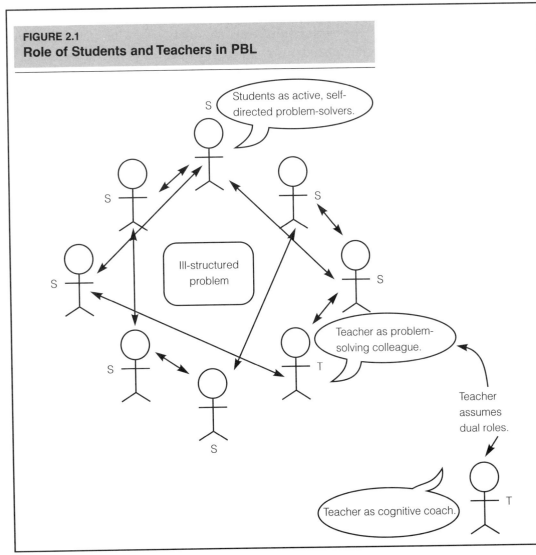

FIGURE 2.1
Role of Students and Teachers in PBL

Students as active, self-directed problem-solvers.

Ill-structured problem

Teacher as problem-solving colleague.

Teacher assumes dual roles.

Teacher as cognitive coach.

p. 123). Which perspective will intrigue students and provide the greatest opportunity for engagement? We want students to own the problem and the inquiry, and make a personal investment in the solution.

A shift in perspective can profoundly affect problem resolution. Imagine how different the problem of the endangered spotted owl in old growth forests in the Pacific Northwest appears from the perspective of legislator, lumberman, environmentalist, and retailer in a local community.

Unit development also includes selecting appropriate information and community resources, and creating materials to support student learning.

Problem Implementation

Planning for instruction requires an appreciation of the teaching and learning events of PBL, along with an understanding of the teacher's role as cognitive coach. Through hundreds of classroom observations, we have found several events that are essential for successful PBL experiences. As teachers construct a teaching and learning template, they have clear goals for each event, and the goals support student thinking at different levels. As teachers coach students toward these goals, they anticipate embedding essential instruction and assessment at critical points during problem investigation. We detail these teaching and learning events in Chapter 4, but for now, let's consider the natural flow of problem-based learning as students meet, investigate, and resolve a problem.

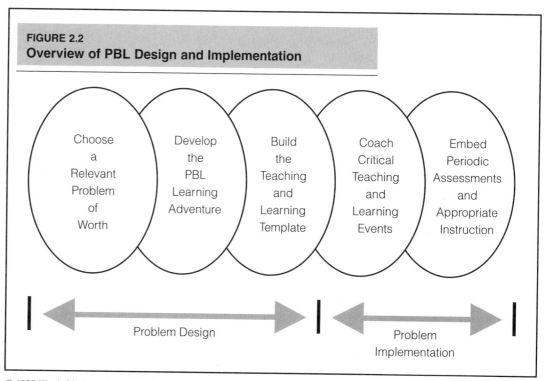

FIGURE 2.2
Overview of PBL Design and Implementation

Choose a Relevant Problem of Worth

Develop the PBL Learning Adventure

Build the Teaching and Learning Template

Coach Critical Teaching and Learning Events

Embed Periodic Assessments and Appropriate Instruction

Problem Design

Problem Implementation

The Flow of a PBL Learning Experience

Students assume the role of a stakeholder in the problem scenario. We want our learners to get inside the learning situation and own the problem. It is important that their role be one in which they will naturally have some say in the outcome or resolution. If they are to make recommendations to the mayor about traffic flow during a major event in their city, which role would provide them a greater voice or influence? Members of the Department of Transportation? Downtown retailers? Middle school students?

That is not to say that students should shift roles for every problem. What if their school needs major renovation and a building addition? Who better to examine the school's physical environment in relation to the learning needs of middle grade students, and to make recommendations to the architect and school board? What is important is that the role and situation are complementary and provide a platform for influencing the outcome.

We also want students to make an empathic connection with the situation; in other words, we want them to care about what happens. Sylwester (1995) states:

> We know emotion is very important to the educative process because it drives attention, which drives learning and memory (p. 72).

Later he goes on to say:

> By separating emotion from logic and reason in the classroom, we've simplified school management and evaluation, but we've also then separated two sides of one coin—and lost something important in the process (p. 75).

Students are immersed in an ill-structured problematic situation. Such a situation is messy and complex. Not enough information is provided, so the situation requires inquiry, information gathering, and reflection. As information is gathered and evaluated, what was thought to be the root problem or puzzlement may change, opening up new avenues for investigation. Students uncover diverging assumptions, conflicting evidence, and varying opinions about the situation. Even when students decide upon a solution, there are probably multiple options for achieving it. A problematic situation is changing, tentative, and has no simple or fixed solution.

Why, then, do we center PBL around these types of problems? Matthew Lipman (1991) in *Thinking in Education* makes a strong argument in favor of ill-structured problems:

> Where students have no sense that anything has been left out or is incomplete, they have no need to go beyond the information given. In contrast, the partial, the fragmentary, and the problematic taunt us to complete them or resolve them (p. 68).

Students must analyze, synthesize, and evaluate to gain a sense of the whole and formulate a viable solution. Well-structured problems, on the other hand, provide the information, the compass, and a clear destination for the problem solver, tapping only the lower-level thinking skills of knowledge, comprehension, and application.

What does such work mean for younger students? Do we hold back PBL experiences until children near middle school age? Not at all. Primary grade students engage in PBL scenarios with a vigor and enthusiasm that surprises and delights their teachers. These children are not limited by the notion that all information is located between the covers of an encyclopedia. They pursue information by phoning, questioning, and experimenting. Like good investigators, they know the value of probing beyond first-level answers by asking "Why?" again and again and again. Problematic scenarios appropriate for younger students abound. Just as beauty lies in the eye of the beholder, what makes something a problem resides in the mind of the learner.

For example, a problem scenario described in Chapter 1 explains how 1st graders were enlisted to help their principal solve the mystery of why her garden wouldn't grow properly. They learned more about plants, growth, and conditions for life than they would have from any story and windowsill garden. What's more important, they experienced the critical connection between learning and life.

Students identify what they know and need to know. From what they know of their role, the situation, and the limited information provided, students clarify and share what they know. This process helps them access prior knowledge and begin to make connections. The ill-structured problem compels students to identify what they know and need to know to resolve the tension of a problem situation (Boud and Feletti 1991). Almost concurrently, they begin to understand the situation more fully. From this point, a natural progression occurs to categorize information needs and potential sources while parceling out tasks.

Teachers may be concerned about students taking a wrong turn or going down a blind alley as they plan or gather information. Students will, on occasion, do just that. But in doing so, they will undoubtedly learn from the experience. Often, knowing what doesn't work or apply in a given situation is every bit as valuable as knowing what does. The messiness of authentic problem solving—including an occasionally seemingly nonproductive detour—yields rich learning:

> Students in a summer youth program worked at an area forest preserve. In years past, they were given explicit directions about the building and placement of bat houses within the preserve. Following a shift to a PBL program frame, students were challenged to accomplish the same goal, but this time, they investigated the native bats and their habitat, designed the bat houses, and placed them appropriately. Despite this need for

inquiry coupled with predictable meandering, these students accomplished a great deal more with noticeable interest and enthusiasm when the goal was problemized as compared to when the goals were explicit (Benoit 1996).

Students define the problem to focus further investigation. Once students are immersed in their role and the problematic situation, they gather and share information among the other class members or their team. This activity enables all to gain a holistic understanding of the problem. Collecting information often takes on a life of its own—intriguing threads are followed, personal interests take over, and the inquiry becomes blurred. Coaching students to come to a clear statement of what they believe to be the central issue of the problem, along with a list of several conditions that need to be satisfied for a good solution, is essential. Many teachers with whom we work post evolving problem statements in the classroom to help tighten and target the investigation.

It is likely that students will engage in more than one cycle of inquiry—sharing what they have discovered, identifying what else they need to know, and refining their problem statement as they learn more—before they are ready to consider some sort of resolution. Motivated by their inquiry, students become self-directed learners. A key is to interest them in the learning experience:

> Teaching is generally a delightful experience when we focus on activities that student brains enjoy doing and do well, such as exploring concepts, creating

metaphors, estimating and predicting, cooperating on group tasks, and discussing moral or ethical issues (Sylwester 1995, p. 119).

Students generate several possible solutions and identify the one that fits best. With appropriate coaching, they discuss an emerging picture of the real problem, perhaps several times before they are ready to generate possible solutions. After developing the solutions, they evaluate them in light of the problem statement's central issue and identified conditions. According to Sylwester (1995), the brain is well suited for this type of activity:

> Our brain is currently much better than a computer at conceptualizing ambiguous problems—at identifying definitive and value-laden elements that it can incorporate into an acceptable general solution (p. 119).

Once students select the solution that fits best, they prepare to present their findings. They may choose to share the problem and their solution by using concept maps, charts, graphs, proposals, position papers, memos, maps, models, videos, or a home page on the World Wide Web—whatever is authentic to their role and the situation. Students offer this solution in a performance assessment situation, ideally interacting with the problem's real stakeholders and responding to stakeholder questions and concerns. If appropriate, these stakeholders may even implement the solution.

For example, students at Steinmetz High School in Chicago were participants in a problem-based service learning project. They identified a problem within their community at a local hospital. The hospital had recently located some biohazardous waste that had been stored since the 1930s. The students took on the problem and investigated the legal, ethical, waste management, and health concerns inherent in this problem. They arrived at a viable solution and presented it to the hospital board. The board adopted their proposal.

As a thinking and learning process, problem-based learning empowers students as learners and doers to translate imagination and thought into actuality as well as to reflect on the process and proposed solution.

What Are the Essential Elements of Problem-Based Learning?

Many formats for presenting and implementing PBL units are possible; however, the following parameters remain consistent:

 The problematic situation is presented first and serves as the organizing center and context for learning.

 The problematic situation has common characteristics:
- It is ill-structured and messy.
- It often changes with the addition of new information.
- It is not solved easily or with a specific formula.
- It does not result in one right answer.

Students are active problem solvers and learners; teachers are cognitive and metacognitive coaches.

 Information is shared, but knowledge is a personal construction of the learner. Discussion and challenge expose and test thinking.

 Assessment is an authentic companion to the problem and process.

 A PBL unit is not necessarily interdisciplinary, but it is always integrative.

What Are the Benefits of Problem-Based Learning?

Although PBL plays out differently in varying settings, from primary to graduate classrooms, particular benefits have surfaced at all levels. At the Illinois Mathematics and Science Academy (IMSA), a core group of teachers has designed and implemented problem-based learning units and courses since the early 1990s. Their experiences and reflections coupled with findings from the research literature present a profile of PBL's benefits (see Gallagher, Rosenthal, and Stepien 1992; Stepien and Gallagher 1993). We highlight the benefits here and provide supporting teacher comments describing their experiences with PBL.

Increases Motivation

PBL engages students in learning through the attraction or pull of problem dissonance or tension. They take on more and delve deeper as they make a personal investment in the outcome of their inquiry. Teacher comments attest to this involvement:

> The most important thing that happened to me is that when I got involved in doing problem-based learning, it was so obvious to me—the difference in the way in which students approached their own responsibilities and activities in the classroom compared to the way students did when I used other methods. . . . They just did different things. I think it was important to me to *see* that they did different things, because it was clear to me that for their learning to change they *had* to do different things.
>
> —David Workman, Science/Physics Teacher
> Illinois Mathematics and Science Academy, Aurora, Ill.

> It's so much more exciting to see real learning going on. And it's real—you know, where the kids are really hungry to learn. A kid came back up to me the next day and said, "I went over to the city library and checked out *Uncle Tom's Cabin* on my own." He didn't act like it was a big thing; I thought it was pretty amazing! That book is 140 years old or something, and he was wading through it.
>
> —Kris Hightshoe, Social Studies Teacher
> Edison Middle School, Champaign, Ill.

Makes Learning Relevant to the Real World

PBL offers students an obvious answer to the questions, "Why do we need to learn this information?" and "What does what I am doing in school have to do with anything in the real world?" Teacher comments show how learning relevant material in schools affects students:

> The last two days, I've had my students out doing orienteering. They really enjoyed it. Now in hindsight, I see that problem-based learning is a lot like orienteering through a problem. What I discovered was that I would get them going and they would scurry into the woods with their compasses and try to find the various answers or points that they were seeking. . . . When they came back, there was this great rejoicing in their own accomplishment. I can't imagine how I could have explained it or the kind of lecture I would have had to give to explain those points in the woods that would have received the same kind of reaction as their actually doing it. . . . There was a problem; the problem was that they find [the point]; when they found it, it was like they had beaten the system. The woods had not beaten them. To me that's not a bad comparison to what problem-based [learning] is. You go into the wilderness and once you find those things, there is a joy of discovery. I don't know that the joy of being told is nearly as great.
> —John Thompson, Science/Biology Teacher
> Illinois Mathematics and Science Academy, Aurora, Ill.

> Suddenly the students have real tasks to do and real reasons to want to learn about things. People are taking them seriously as learners; it's not just a mock situation.
> —Lori Hinton, 4th/5th Grade Teacher
> Westgate Elementary School, Arlington Heights, Ill.

Promotes Higher-Order Thinking

Coupled with cognitive coaching strategies, the ill-structured problem scenario calls upon critical and creative thinking by suspending the guessing game of, "What's the right answer the teacher wants me to find?" Students gather information significant to the problem, assessing its credibility and validity. In bringing the problem to acceptable closure with evidence to support decisions, students are held to high benchmarks of thinking. Teachers work to encourage such thinking:

> We've had some panels of experts come in and hear solutions from our groups. The adults are just astounded by the depth and breadth of their knowledge and the kinds of things they've been able to deal with. Even experts came in as resources, thinking they were going to give a canned speech and left [only] five minutes for questions. I said, "Excuse me, but could you present for five minutes, and then we'll have an hour of questions?" . . . The kids are asking incredibly complex questions that show they have a lot of understanding of content.
> —Louise Robb, Language Arts Teacher,
> Barrington Middle School, Prairie Campus,
> Barrington, Ill.

> You've got to get used to being able to reflect back the question—bounce it right back—rather than feel the necessity to give the answer. That's not easy to do.
> —Richard Dods, Science/Chemistry Teacher
> Illinois Mathematics and Science Academy, Aurora, Ill.

Encourages Learning How to Learn

PBL promotes metacognition and self-regulated learning as students generate strategies for problem definition, information gathering, data analysis, and hypothesis building and testing—and share and compare those strategies with those of other students and mentors. Such challenging work goes on at all grade levels:

> I think it's critical for a kid to be able to formulate the process: "That's what I know and that's what I need to know." If they can begin to think about how they are thinking that way, they could know either where to get the stuff or add to whatever they know. . . . They are much more adaptable—now I'm going to start talking like an ecologist here—but their ability to adapt to whatever intellectual or challenging environment they are put in, is lots better—was it Pasteur who said, "Chance favors the prepared mind"? The question is, How do you prepare the mind? Is it simply by knowing more stuff? Or knowing how to approach the problem?
> —John Thompson, Science/Biology Teacher
> Illinois Mathematics and Science Academy, Aurora, Ill.

> First-graders are not inhibited. They're ready to hit the phones, go on the Internet, go ask their neighbors. They are open to inquiry, and they're not afraid of that challenge. They're able to define for themselves aspects of the work that interest and challenge them. . . . It's a whole new way for these kids to not just be able to think, but to do.
> —Emily Alford, Former Principal
> Westgate Elementary School, Arlington Heights, Ill.

Requires Authenticity

PBL engages student learning in ways that are similar to real-world situations and assesses learning in ways that demonstrate understanding and not mere replication. Teachers report on the results of providing authentic situations and assessment:

> It wasn't clear to me how powerful the method was until almost two-thirds of the way through that first year, when it became obvious that significant groups of kids were taking off totally on their own and going in powerful directions that we had hoped would occur, but weren't guaranteed would occur. And the kids kept coming to us and saying that this is the way it ought to be. They were doing things that were just astonishing. I still remember—[a student]—who went off to the conference on the West Coast. She became . . . in a year one of the prime experts on ELF (electromagnetic low frequency) fields and biological systems in the country. She knew as much as the experts.
> —David Workman, Science/Physics Teacher
> Illinois Mathematics and Science Academy, Aurora, Ill.

> Simulated problems certainly can have value, but how can you compare a simulation with the power of real-world problem solving that has genuine results? Some of my students were able to convince a previously adamantly opposed village board to allow a pilot run for a local dance club, while others developed a Web site and brochure for a local pet shelter to help it gain needed publicity.
> —Ellen Jo Ljung, Language Arts Teacher
> Glenbard West High School, Glen Ellyn, Ill.

A Landscape of Instructional Strategies

In thinking about the benefits of PBL and students as knowers, thinkers, and doers, we have chosen to differentiate problem-based learning from a range of instructional strategies. We know that each strategy has its place in a teacher's instructional repertoire, and we see clear differences when considering the role of the student, teacher, and problem, along with other key factors (see Figure 2.3).

Summary

We have described what problem-based learning is and how it develops student dispositions toward inquiry and decision making based on evidence, not assertion. Both from the literature and our experience, we know that in PBL, students gather and apply knowledge and skills from multiple disciplines and sources as they assess an array of plausible solutions for a relevant ill-structured problem. In the next chapter, we delve into the background of PBL and examine how PBL enables students to emerge as open-minded, adaptable, complex thinkers able creatively and critically to assess the ever-changing world around them.

FIGURE 2.3
Comparison of Instructional Strategies

Type of Instruction	Role of the Teacher	Role of the Student	Cognitive Focus	Metacognitive Focus	Role in the Problem	Problem	Information
Lecture	As expert: • Directs thinking • Holds knowledge • Evaluates students	As receiver: • Inert • Inactive • Empty	Students replicate received knowledge and apply in testing situation.	None: Study skills are the responsibility of the student.	As a student: Learns about things outside personal experience or "over there" (Heathcote and Herbert 1980).	• Well structured • Presented as a challenge to retention	Organized and presented by instructor.
Direct Instruction	As conductor: • Orchestrates learning • Guides rehearsal • Evaluates students	As follower: • Responsive • Semi-active • Waits for teacher's lead	Students practice and replicate received knowledge and apply in testing situation.	Guided practice provides tacit focus upon strategies.	As a student: Learns about things outside personal experience or "over there" (Heathcote and Herbert 1980).	• Well structured • Presented as a challenge to retention	Organized and presented by instructor.
Case Method	As consultant: • Lectures • Sets the environment • Advises • Evaluates students	As client: • Responsive • Semi-active • Applies own experience	Students apply received knowledge and own experience in case resolution.	Strategies learned are applied to cases, not necessarily independently.	As a student: Learns about things outside personal experience or "over there" (Heathcote and Herbert 1980).	• Well structured • Presented as a challenge to application and analysis	Most is organized and presented by instructor.
Discovery-Based Inquiry	As mystery writer: • Combines parts that lead to discovery • Provides clues and foreshadows events • Evaluates students	As detective: • Picks up clues • Semi-active • Seeks out evidence	Students apply "discovered" truths to the construction of other constructs and principles.	Inquiry process learned is applied to investigations, not necessarily independently.	As a student: Learns about things outside personal experience or "over there" (Heathcote and Herbert 1980).	• Well structured • Presented as a strategy for knowledge construction	Most is organized and presented by instructor.
Problem-Centered Learning	As resource: • Explicitly teaches content and problem solving • Poses problems to which students relate • Translates into students' world • Evaluates students	As problem solver: • Evaluates resources • Crafts divergent solutions • Active	Students synthesize received knowledge and individuality in the resolution of problems within curricular context.	Problem-solving process learned is applied to problems, not necessarily independently.	As a student: Learns about things outside personal experience or "over there" (Heathcote and Herbert 1980).	• Moderately structured • Presented as a strategy to develop effective learning behaviors	Most is organized and presented by instructor.

FIGURE 2.3—*CONTINUED*
Comparison of Instructional Strategies

TYPE OF INSTRUCTION	ROLE OF THE TEACHER	ROLE OF THE STUDENT	COGNITIVE FOCUS	METACOGNITIVE FOCUS	ROLE IN THE PROBLEM	PROBLEM	INFORMATION
Simulation and Gaming	As stage manager: • Manages situation • Sets simulation/ game in motion • Watches from the wings • Debriefs situation	As player: • Experiences simulation/game • Reacts to emergent conditions/ variables • Active	Students learn about themselves, their roles in life situations, and about the reality modeled.	• Learning exposed during the debriefing process. • Experience interpreted and evaluated in reflection.	As a player or pawn: Reacts to events that are part of personal experience or "here" to relate to things "over there" (Heathcote and Herbert 1980).	• Moderately structured • Presented as a strategy to understand self and events	Most is organized and presented by instructor.
Mantle of the Expert (Roles)	As travel agent: • Enables learning from within group • Maps ways in which students will discover what they need to know to complete task • Guides their journey • Debriefs situation	As traveler: • Actively experiences the journey • Acts within and through a historical perspective	Students reconstruct classroom communication, creating a dialectic where they learn at the conceptual, personal, and social levels.	• The eminent pressure of the lived experience activates prior learning. • Teacher simultaneously models and coaches.	As a doer: Walks in the time of the event, learning about events "here" (Heathcote and Herbert 1980).	• Tightly focused, but somewhat ill-structured • Presented as a situation that demands interaction with the social system	Most is organized and presented by instructor.
Problem-Based Learning	As coach: • Presents problematic situation • Models, coaches, and fades • Engages in the process as coinvestigator • Assesses learning	As participant: • Actively grapples with the complexity of the situation • Investigates and resolves problem from the inside	Students synthesize and construct knowledge to bring resolution to problems in a way that meets the conditions that they themselves set forth.	• Teacher models and coaches as needed. • Students develop strategies to enable and direct their own learning.	As a stakeholder: Immerses in the situation, learning about events "here" (Heathcote and Herbert 1980).	• Ill-structured • Presented as a situation within which a compelling problem is yet to be defined	Little is presented by instructor without students identifying a need to know. Most is gathered and analyzed by students.

References: Alkove and McCarthy 1992; Casey and Tucker 1994; Cornbleth 1988; Doll 1993; Heathcote 1983; Heathcote and Herbert 1980; Lederman 1994; Swink 1993; Wagner 1988; Willems 1981; Wolf, McIlvain, and Stockburger 1992.

3

WHAT ARE THE FOUNDATIONS OF PROBLEM-BASED LEARNING?

STUDENTS LEARN FROM REAL ACTIVITY (GLICKMAN 1991). The simplicity and logic of this statement have been embraced, researched, and written about for nearly a century. PBL is a form of experiential education in which learners think, know, and do in an authentic context. Widely used in medical and business education for several decades, PBL has been used in its present form in K–12 education for several years. But the core of PBL—students as active problem solvers, making their own meaning—is an educational tradition dating back to John Dewey. To understand the foundations of PBL, we turn first to medical education, and then in more depth to PBL's constructivist roots in K–12 education.

Beginnings at the Medical School Level

Problem-based learning as a distinct educational term has its origins in medical education in the 1960s. At that time, clinical medical educators at

McMaster University in Ontario, Canada, became increasingly concerned with a student's ability to recall and apply in clinical settings biomedical content knowledge and skills taught (and presumably learned) in previous biomedical coursework. Learning through lecture did not equate well with application, and grades, although valued indicators of success, were not good predictors of a student's ability to apply that knowledge in clinical situations with real patients (Albanese and Mitchell 1993). It is a situation familiar to us all—reproduce for the test and soon forget.

As a consequence, these educators designed a program that placed students in small tutorial groups where they interacted with simulated patients who had medical problems blurred by patient anxiety, incomplete information, and the frailties of interpersonal communication. They used patient interviews, records, and selected laboratory results to identify learning issues and develop a diagnosis and treatment plan. A discussion-based process that faculty tutors facilitated brought students into the inquiry and learning process as full participants rather than as receptors (Barrows and Tamblyn 1976).

In the 1970s, the University of New Mexico, supported by colleagues from McMaster University, began a small PBL program side by side with the pre-existing traditional program. As comparative evidence mounted, it was clear that the PBL students were learning as much content as the traditional students, thus easing some initial discomfort with coverage issues. Studies also found that students in the new program were less threatened by their environment and more able to pursue learning independently, an indication that they were equipped to be lifelong learners (Aspy, Aspy, and Quinby 1993).

In the 1980s, Harvard University Medical School's New Pathways Program adopted a problem-based learning format for one of its four learning societies of 40 students. The 1990s saw other medical schools moving toward problem-based learning—Southern Illinois University, Rush, Bowman Gray, Tufts, Michigan State, and University of Hawaii, to name a few (Aspy, Aspy, and Quinby 1993).

Problem-based learning in medical schools is supported to a large degree by information-processing theory. The central ideas of this theory are that the learning situation

- Activates prior knowledge, facilitating new learning.
- Parallels ways in which this knowledge will be needed in real-world situations.
- Increases the probability that the learner will recall and apply what is stored in memory.

For students who are to become physicians, their roles and the problematic situations into which they are immersed as learners are clear. There is a direct relationship between learning situations and application situations—students assume the role of doctors attending to the needs of their patients because students will *be* doctors attending to the needs of their patients. As they learn, they accumulate a bank of cues that serve to trigger memory and activate knowledge associated with learning situations. Information processing is an efficient and effective accessing and flow of information (Perkins 1992). Such work, though, does not eliminate the possibility for a great deal of ambiguity and uncertainly in comforting, counseling, and caring for patients. In K–12 settings, we find significant differences when we consider the needs of learners and the psychological foundation we propose for PBL.

Foundations in K–12 Education

We, too, want our students to recall and apply what they have learned, but we cannot predict the setting in which this learning will be applied. Our students may go on to become teachers, engineers, secretaries, programmers, or ? We may never know, but we are charged, nevertheless, with preparing them to face their futures. We also know little about what they know—truly know—when they walk into our classrooms. We must facilitate a wide range of cognitive activity inherent in answering these questions:

- What do our learners bring to the situation?
- What do they do with it?
- What do they walk away with?

In other words, students must do and think. As David Perkins (1992) points out, "If students do not learn to think with the knowledge they are stockpiling, they might as well not have it" (p. 30). To be able to think in that way, students need to understand at deeper levels. And to understand at deeper levels they need to engage in sustained thinking about topics or issues—to crawl inside ideas and expose misconceptions while making multiple connections. From this intimate perspective, students become

knowers and doers and thinkers, adapting and integrating new learning in the process.

Brooks and Brooks (1993) cite Greenberg's (Greenberg 1990) four criteria for a good problem-solving situation as exemplars of a constructivist approach:

- Students make a testable prediction.
- Students can use available or easily accessible materials.
- The situation itself is complex enough to support varied approaches and generate multiple solutions.
- The problem-solving process is enhanced, not hindered, by a collaborative approach.

They extend these with the additional criterion of relevance: Students see a link, whether inherent in the situation or mediated by the teacher, between their situation and the real world. "Posing problems of emerging relevance is a guiding principle of constructivist pedagogy" (Brooks and Brooks 1993, p. 35).

Why Constructivism?

Various professional organizations and groups within education are defining curriculum standards and desired learning outcomes within a more constructivist framework. Such a framework suggests posing relevant problems to learners and structuring learning around primary concepts (for example, in science, see the *National Science Education Standards* [National Research Council 1996] and the

Benchmarks for Science Literacy [American Association for the Advancement of Science, Project 2061 1993]). Other groups define a need for competence in not only basic skills and personal qualities but also thinking skills, such as solving problems, reasoning, and knowing how to learn, for solid work performance (for example, see U.S. Department of Labor 1991).

Such major change in education really involves replacing the whole educational system (Reigeluth 1994). Earlier in this century, when workers needed to be compliant and know how to perform discrete tasks, our bureaucratic, centralized, hierarchical educational system fit the bill. Today, however, in an information age, there is general agreement that people will work in teams in more democratic organizations and will need to be able to take personal initiative and integrate tasks. According to Reigeluth, emerging features for a new educational system for this information age include cooperative learning, thinking, problem-solving skills and meaning making, communication skills, and the teacher as coach or facilitator of learning. These features sound a great deal like the features of problem-based learning.

A Brief Look at Constructivist Theory and Practice

During the Progressive Era, Dewey (1916) saw the tackling of significant problems as the ultimate way to engage learners in meaning making and problem solving. He further believed that learning should be situated within the context of community (Dewey 1943). Interest in such open inquiry, activity-based, and integrative approaches in our classrooms has increased in recent years, and today, these types of approaches are sometimes called constructivism (Brooks and Brooks 1993).

Constructivist Theory

Constructivism is a philosophical view on how we come to understand or know. The idea that knowledge is constructed in the minds of learners is not new, but is today perhaps best characterized by philosopher Richard Rorty (1991). Rorty presents knowledge, not as a representation of the real world or a "match" between knowledge and reality, but rather as a collection of conceptual structures that are adapted, or viable, within a person's range of experience. In other words, the person's knowledge "fits" with the world, much like how a key fits a lock (Bodner 1986). Each of us builds our own key by making sense of the world—and many different keys can open a given lock.

Constructivist theory in education comes primarily from the work of John Dewey and Jean Piaget. Working from this idea that learners construct their own knowledge, both Dewey and Piaget contend that the stimulus for learning is some experience of cognitive conflict, or "puzzlement" (Savery and Duffy 1995). Dewey argued that learning should prepare one for life, not simply for work. He proposed that learning be organized around the interests of the learner and that learning is an active effort by learners interested in resolving particular issues. Piaget proposed that cognitive change and learning take place when a learner's way of thinking, or scheme, instead of producing what the learner expects, leads to perturbation. This perturbation (puzzlement) then leads to accommodation (cognitive change) and a new sense of equilibrium.

Cognitive change often comes about as a result of interactions with other learners who may hold different understandings (von Glasersfeld 1989). These social interactions may challenge our current views as well as allow us to test our current understandings to see how well they help us to make sense of and function in our world (Savery and Duffy 1995). Learners bring their own suppositions to learning experiences based on what fits their experiences. For example, a learner might believe that "nothing is left but the taste" when sugar dissolves in hot water. This supposition will likely hold with that learner unless she can construct a new supposition that more appropriately explains her experience with sugar and water and can be supported with evidence (Bodner 1986).

A Constructivist Educational Model

> Although not a theory of teaching, constructivism is serving as the basis for many of the current reforms in education. . . . This [theory to practice] connection is crucial if the new reforms are to be based on substance rather than faddish practices.
> —Catherine Fosnot, in Brooks and Brooks 1993, p. vii

Here are some recommendations for a constructivist model of learning, based on the work of numerous authors:

- Posing learning around larger tasks or problems relevant to students.
- Structuring learning around primary concepts.
- Supporting the learner working in a complex, authentic environment.
- Seeking and valuing students' points of view.
- Assessing student learning in the context of teaching and incorporating self-assessment.
- Supporting and challenging student thinking through cognitive coaching.
- Encouraging collaborative groups for testing student ideas against alternative views.
- Encouraging the use of alternative and primary sources for information.
- Adapting curriculum to address student questions and ideas.

In a constructivist social science classroom, for example, a high school teacher uses several of the preceding recommendations to plan an experience on how social policies in the 1980s affected the economic and educational profile of the African American population in the United States (Brooks and Brooks 1993). Instead of reading a textbook, students are coached to interpret census reports obtained from the Internet and to generate their own hypotheses about social policies. We work with teachers who use census or other demographic data on a variety of issues, such as characteristics of U.S. presidents, or data on cases of the plague in the 20th century, as the stimulus for learning and meaning making in their classes.

Constructivism and Problem-Based Learning

Problem-based learning may be one of the best exemplars of a constructivist learning environment (Savery and Duffy 1995). The design of engaging, ill-structured problem scenarios for K–12 students, which is described in Chapter 4, exemplifies several important constructivist principles. Brooks and Brooks (1993) stress the importance of centering learning around such problems:

> We realized that the nature of questions posed to students greatly influences the depth to which the students search for answers. Posing problems of emerging relevance and searching for windows into students' thinking form a particular frame of reference about the role of the teacher and about the teaching process. It cannot be included in a teacher's repertoire as an add-on. It must be a basic element of that repertoire (p. 44).

Implementing PBL in K–12 classrooms requires teachers to assume the role of coach and students to be active learners and problem solvers. As teachers model and coach strong cognitive and metacognitive behaviors and dispositions, students learn how to learn and become excited about learning through problem solving. Von Glasersfeld

(1993) indicates that we can show students that there is profound satisfaction in thinking one's way to a solution and that this satisfaction can generate the motivation to learn more.

Assessing student learning in PBL is always done in the context of the problematic situation. Such assessment is designed for teachers to monitor the thinking and dispositions of the student and to subsequently adjust the learning experience, or as Brooks and Brooks (1993) put it, "Assessment and teaching [are] merged in service to the learner" (p. 91). We could also think of such assessment as developing a "model" of the student (von Glasersfeld 1993) in which teachers get an idea of the conceptual structures in the students' heads so they may better teach students to learn. Finally, assessment serves the important purpose of evaluating student attainment of significant outcomes identified for the PBL experience.

Summary

PBL is a powerful strategy for curriculum, instruction, and assessment. It has rich foundations both in experiential learning theory and philosophy and at the professional school level. Having laid this foundation, we proceed in the next chapters to explore PBL in more detail in K–12 education. We examine the teaching and learning events in PBL, the design of PBL experiences, and the implementation of PBL in real classrooms.

4

WHAT IS OUR MODEL FOR PROBLEM-BASED LEARNING?

DURING THE PAST FIVE YEARS, WE HAVE DESIGNED AND developed PBL units and courses, shared our experiences with educators and PBL experts around the world, and engaged in research to describe and assess the effects of PBL in K–12 education. Such work has informed our thinking and contributed to a picture of PBL as practiced in K–12 settings. This model of the important processes of PBL—design and implementation—fits well with a constructivist model of teaching and learning. Just how does it fit? This chapter outlines our model of the teaching and learning events in PBL.

Teaching and Learning Events in PBL

The teaching and learning events are designed to promote active student learning. They generate important learning issues around a carefully crafted problem situation so that students can work through the issues in authentic and rigorous ways. These events are not necessarily rigid, fixed, or strictly sequenced. Learners may revisit parts of the PBL process, particularly *defining the problem statement and gathering and sharing information* (described in this chapter), as they delve deeper into the problem. A colleague, Bernard Hollister, likens the process to "stripping away the layers of the onion":

> As learners explore the problem, their knowledge base increases as they find new and different sources of information about the problem. Of course, a learner could stop at any layer of the problem and offer solutions. It is the job of the teacher/coach to push learners to keep stripping away the layers of the onion so that the learners are not comfortable with just simplistic problem statements.
> —Bernard Hollister, Social Science Teacher
> Illinois Mathematics and Science Academy, Aurora, Ill.

In Hollister's comments, we also hear evidence of the critical role that the teacher/coach plays in problem-based learning. As we stated in Chapter 2 (and will undoubtedly state again), problem-based learning is composed of two complementary processes. It is both a model for curriculum organization and an instructional strategy; the two go hand in hand. Figure 4.1 shows the instructional strategy component, including the teaching and learning events essential for PBL experiences.

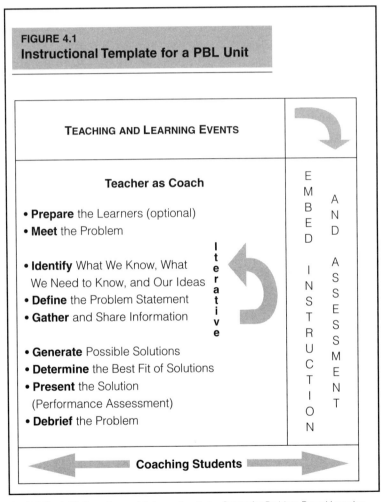

FIGURE 4.1
Instructional Template for a PBL Unit

TEACHING AND LEARNING EVENTS

Teacher as Coach

- **Prepare** the Learners (optional)
- **Meet** the Problem

- **Identify** What We Know, What We Need to Know, and Our Ideas
- **Define** the Problem Statement
- **Gather** and Share Information

- **Generate** Possible Solutions
- **Determine** the Best Fit of Solutions
- **Present** the Solution (Performance Assessment)
- **Debrief** the Problem

Iterative

EMBED INSTRUCTION AND ASSESSMENT

Coaching Students

In this chapter, to highlight the PBL teaching and learning events, we use a particular PBL learning experience centered on overpopulation of mosquitoes in a suburban area. Although this problem was designed as a professional development immersion experience (Center for Problem-Based Learning 1996c), it has also been used in middle and high school classrooms. We frame our problem around the role and situation into which the learner will be placed and an articulation of the problem statement we believe will drive inquiry and generate solutions:

Role and Situation

A fictitious county, Center County, is confronted with an explosion in the mosquito population. The Center County Manager, Richard Clarke, alerts the Center County Mosquito Abatement Agency to the concerns of the citizenry. Learners assume the role of community members selected for an advisory panel to the Center County Mosquito Abatement Agency. These members generate varying theories about the cause and investigate potential solutions to the problem.

Anticipated Problem Statement

How can we, as members of the advisory panel, determine the cause of the mosquito population problem and recommend a possible solution in such a way that we consider all the relevant factors—health, social, environmental, political, and financial?

Preparing the Learners

Goal: Support learners as they encounter problem-based learning.

This support may take very different forms, depending on such variables as the age of the learners, their interests and background, and the nature of the problem. A primary grade teacher prepared her students for a PBL experience about growing healthy plants by setting up several plant experiments students could observe and discuss (like a celery stalk absorbing colored water); putting out books related to plants in the reading area; and practicing the KWL strategy with her students (What do I know? What do I want to know? What have I learned?).

Two middle school teachers who team teach using PBL prepare their students each year through team building, critical thinking activities, and creativity exercises. Other teachers choose to conduct a simulation-type experience or a small-scale, problem-based experience with students (two or three hours and less ill-structured) before they begin a lengthier, more complex PBL experience.

One area to avoid when preparing students is teaching the content of the problem before you get started. PBL is distinguished from other types of experiential education because students learn the content and skills *in* the course of solving the problem. The appropriate amount and type of preparation—whether touching on content or processes encountered in the problem—must be determined based on the needs and experiences of your learners. Students who have encountered PBL several times may not need any specific preparation before meeting a problem.

Here is how we prepare the learners for problem solving in our mosquito problem:
- Learners reflect on a real problem they have dealt with; as a small group, we brainstorm about the problem-solving process we use when we encounter problems.
- Learners watch a brief video clip from the movie *Apollo 13* in which the astronauts encounter the problem of the explosion in the rocket's oxygen tank.

Meeting the Problem

Goal: Support learners to develop a personal stake in the problem and to motivate them to want to solve it.

Sometimes, to afford students this stake and motivation, we place them in a role other than that of student (e.g., engineer, consultant, or concerned citizen) so they may engage in the problem authentically. Who would actually be concerned about this problem? Who would have something to gain or lose if the situation were resolved in a particular way?

We can design meeting the problem in a number of ways to engage or hook students. One way we and our partner teachers often use is giving students an authentic-looking letter or document in their role in the problem. The document introduces the problem briefly and gives enough detail so that students can make an initial attempt at defining it.

Another way students may meet a problem is by identifying or enlisting someone who will ask the students to help solve a problem that person is concerned with, such as a principal asking primary grade students to help determine why plants in her garden are not growing well. Teachers have also designed brief dramatic skits to introduce a problem; for example, two high school students may act out an argument that escalates into abuse to introduce middle school students (now genetic consultants) to a problem dealing with the possible genetic causes of aggression. A video clip, newspaper article, notice from a public agency, or phone message recording can also be used.

In the mosquito problem, the learners met the problem through a memo, shown in Figure 4.2.

Identifying What We Know, What We Need to Know, and Our Ideas

Goals
- Support learners in developing an awareness of what they know and need to know, and what ideas they have about the situation.

- Activate learners' prior knowledge about the problematic situation.

- Provide focus for preparing to gather information needed to solve the problem.

This event allows learners to understand the problem and prompts them to investigate relevant subjects and eventually suggest how to bring the problem to an acceptable resolution. Teachers coach students to probe what students know from meeting the problem as well as what knowledge students bring from their experiences. Students document this information on a "know" chart or paper. The "need to knows" are issues the students believe are critical to finding out more about the problem; again, these are recorded. The "need to knows" typically drive students' initial information-gathering efforts. Student "ideas" may relate to how to locate information, or to hunches they have about what may be causing the problem or what may be part of the solution. This event is repeated as needed as students continue to gather new information that may change what they know—and may raise new need-to-know questions and ideas. Figure 4.3 (see p. 38) is a chart showing examples in the three areas for the mosquito problem.

Defining the Problem Statement

Goal: Support learners in stating the overriding issue or problem in the circumstances they have encountered, and in identifying a subset of conflicting conditions that must be served by a good solution.

For the problem statement, we often use the prompt, "How can we . . . in such a way that . . . ." to help pull together the problem and the conditions within which we must solve it. As most of us know from our work and per-

sonal lives, attempting to solve a problem is difficult unless we understand what the problem is, and how much of it we can actually affect.

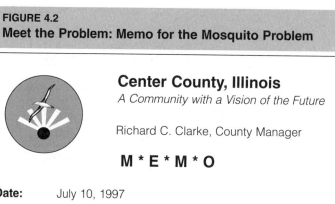

FIGURE 4.2
Meet the Problem: Memo for the Mosquito Problem

Center County, Illinois
A Community with a Vision of the Future

Richard C. Clarke, County Manager

M * E * M * O

Date: July 10, 1997
To: Center County Mosquito Abatement Agency Staff
From: Richard C. Clarke
Subject: Increase in the Mosquito Population

As you can see from the attached newspaper item, residents of Center County are under siege from a population of mosquitoes—possibly the largest ever. The usual mosquito control methods seem to be ineffective in reducing this unprecedented outbreak. Determine the cause of this outbreak and recommend appropriate solutions. I will expect to hear from you on the afternoon of July 17, 1997. In the meantime, I will contact the state to obtain the necessary additional funds to implement the best solution.

Source: Center for Problem-Based Learning 1996c.

The first problem statement from one group working on the mosquito problem was, How can we find a way to return the county's mosquito population to normal so that we do the following:

- Consider environmental impact (livability, biodiversity, and populations).
- Reduce health risks.
- Prevent the problem from happening again.
- Keep costs reasonable.

FIGURE 4.3
A Sample of What We Know, What We Need to Know, and Our Ideas About the Mosquito Problem

Know	Need to Know	Ideas
We need to find causes to mosquito problem in Center County. We must have solutions in a week. Mosquitoes can travel up to 30–40 miles. Rainfall was normal this year.	Geography of entire county. Are these mosquitoes indigenous to this area? Conditions that make mosquitoes thrive. Budget. Have drainage patterns changed recently?	Maybe there is a lot of standing water in the area. Maybe a natural occurrence (like fallen trees) has created standing water. The mosquitoes are resistant to current spraying through mutation or adaptation.

Defining (or refining) the problem statement is revisited as information that may change learners' understanding of the nature of the problem is gathered and shared. For example, the preceding problem statement was later revised by the group: "How can we control the mosquito population in Center County. . . ." This focus is quite different from "return the county's mosquito population to normal."

Learners may also map the problem as it presents itself—making hunches about the potential causes, solutions, and consequences. Figure 4.4 shows a map for the mosquito problem.

Gathering and Sharing Information

Goals
- Support learners in planning and implementing effective information gathering, sharing, and meaning-making strategies.
- Support learners in understanding how new information contributes to understanding the problem, and how information is evaluated in light of its contribution to that understanding.
- Support learners in interpersonal communication and collaborative learning, which contribute to effective problem solving.

Learners typically work in collaborative groups of three to five, organized around particular "need to knows" they have selected. When information gathering is complete,

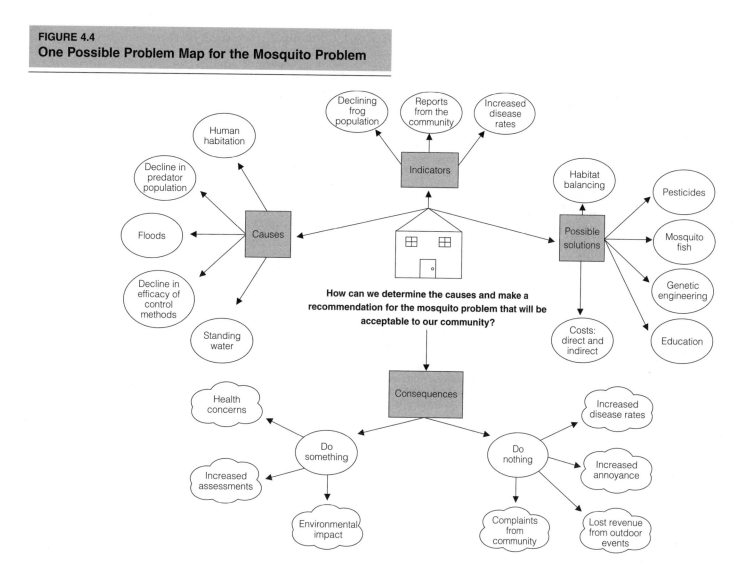

FIGURE 4.4
One Possible Problem Map for the Mosquito Problem

Source: Center for Problem-Based Learning 1996c.

these topic groups are often "jigsawed" (new groups are formed with one person from each topic group, so each can share information gathered). This part of PBL often takes the most time, depending on the problem's complexity, and probably requires the most sophisticated coaching and questioning skills from teachers. Teachers usually determine this event to be complete when students are no longer finding pertinent, new information or when a deadline requires learners to solve the problem with whatever information they have at that point.

Students often have difficulty locating any information, or they find such an abundance, much of it irrelevant, that they may initially struggle. For example, contacting experts on the telephone or asking for price information on plant fertilizer may be new experiences. Some may locate large amounts of information on the Internet, yet not be able to determine what information is most pertinent to the problem. Others may argue over who should do what in their collaborative groups.

After several PBL experiences, teachers learn how to coach students through these difficulties, and students learn to assess themselves and their groups on how well they are gathering and sharing information. Maintaining a focus on the problem statement is helpful in determining what information is needed and most useful.

In the mosquito problem, learners
- Read and discuss information from the Internet on varieties of mosquitoes and different types of mosquito control provided by the agency.

- Check local and state policy in an agency brochure and a manual on state mosquito control.
- Determine whether other resources, such as conflicting viewpoints on the usefulness of biological controls, are accurate and pertinent.
- Ask questions about local conditions, such as population shifts and land use in the affected area.

Generating Possible Solutions

Goal: Support learners in articulating *the full range* of possible options for addressing the problem they have defined.

Again, going back to the problem statement, particularly the conditions for solving the problem, learners begin to recommend solutions based on the information they have gathered.

One useful tool is a decision-making matrix. Figure 4.5 shows an excerpt from a matrix for the mosquito problem.

Determining the Best Fit of Solutions

Goal: Support learners in using the benchmarks of good thinking to evaluate the benefits and consequences of each solution.

The students' goal is to create the most acceptable set of outcomes in response to the conditions specified in the problem statement. This event is crucial to producing a well-supported and feasible solution. Critical thinking literature (for example, see Lipman 1988, Norris 1985) supports the fact that skillful, responsible thinking comes about from good judgment supported by criteria, context, self-correction, and explicit reasons for drawing a conclusion. Students have to balance needs and risks, assess the feasibility of options, and consider which solution gets them closer to their idealized solution.

In the mosquito problem, learners evaluated several possible solutions, including education, chemical application, and further research. A particular group determined that the solution that fit best was a combination of education, chemical application, and research.

Presenting the Solution (Performance Assessment)
Goal: Support learners in effectively articulating and demonstrating what they know, how they know it, and why and for whom knowing is important.

FIGURE 4.5
Excerpt from a Decision-Making Matrix for the Mosquito Problem

Strategy	Pros	Cons	Consequences
Education Free public service announcement. Speak to community groups. Press releases. Content: health issues/risk, prevention, comfort, current treatment.	Low cost. Additional state funds available. Donations. Informed citizens. Lifesaving.	People may think the agency is not doing enough. Fear? Lack of interest?	Change people's minds and behavior. Potentially help reduce mosquito problem. Breeds tolerance and understanding of the bigger ecosystem picture.
Chemical Application	Additional state funds available. Donation.	High cost Safety?	?

Often teachers arrange for outside experts whom students have consulted or others knowledgeable about the problem issues to serve on a panel to assess recommendations and challenge assumptions when students present their solutions. For example, in a middle school problem about a restored prairie on the school campus that was not being maintained properly, the panel consisted of the original landscape architect, district maintenance and grounds personnel, the district business manager, a local environmentalist, and a school board member. A typical format is that several groups from the class present solutions (often very different), and the panel members question each group after its presentation. Assessing this culminating performance is usually conducted using a detailed rubric—often codeveloped by the teacher and students—on content, presentation skills, teamwork, and fit of solution.

Often, as we have observed, most student learning occurs here. Learners hear another group giving details or reasons they had not considered, or offering incorrect information. Panel members ask questions students are not prepared for in initial PBL experiences. Through these challenges, students learn how to present more thoroughly thought-out and well-supported solutions, and to consider the perspective of other stakeholders or their audience in what information is most important. Students become adept at developing visuals to accompany their presentation and in explaining why they are presenting their particular solution.

> In the mosquito problem, learners in four working groups presented their solution to a representative of the county manager (who had asked them to work on the problem). Peer groups assessed solutions and presentations using common criteria. Here is the groups' solution:
>
> We find the best solution to be a combination of education, chemical application, and research.

> Education is the least expensive and perhaps most effective alternative to prevent more problems, reassure area citizens, and make them aware of the agency's current policies and treatments. Limited chemical application, in this crisis situation, is also appropriate, using additional state funding available. Finally, we support further research by agency staff to determine why this outbreak of nonfloodwater mosquitoes is occurring at this time.

Although presentations, poster sessions, and reports offer rich opportunities to evaluate student learning, we also advocate ongoing embedded assessments. These periodic, in-process assessments can take many forms—such as status reports, responses to phone messages from problem stakeholders, mind maps, and problem statements. Whatever forms are used, they provide valuable snapshots of learning that can inform midcourse corrections in the run of a problem and diagnose learning difficulties.

Debriefing the Problem

Goal: For learners to reflect together on what they have learned.

Learners review the effectiveness of the strategies they used and consider what they might do differently in another problem situation. They discuss issues still unresolved or open to further investigation. Sometimes follow-up, particularly in a problem actually occurring in the community, will occur until other stakeholders have resolved the issues. These cognitive and metacognitive strategies—thinking, and thinking about our own learning—are important not only for holding to benchmarks of good thinking, but also for providing a sense of completion to learners who have become personally invested in the problem. They need a realistic awareness of the impact their recommended solutions will have in resolving the problem.

For debriefing the mosquito problem, we had a whole-group discussion in which we discussed the entire PBL experience and what we had learned about ourselves as learners. We also designed a journal entry. Figure 4.6 is a sample of learners' responses.

Summary

Through the teaching and learning events in PBL, students construct knowledge revolving around a relevant problematic situation in a rigorous, thoughtful, connected way. We agree with Savery and Duffy (1995): PBL exemplifies a constructivist model for education, which serves to best prepare our students for life in today's and tomorrow's world. In the next chapter, we help you begin to develop your own PBL curriculum.

FIGURE 4.6
Journal Entry for Debriefing the Mosquito Problem

1. *Describe your response to this problem as a learner. What were you thinking, feeling, and valuing?*
   - I found it interesting having to find a solution to a complex problem with limited and sometimes contradictory information and with not very much time (real life).
   - I was thinking of the importance of the information you receive in defining the strategy for attacking a problem.
   - I learned a lot about the different kinds of mosquitoes and how they attack and where they live. The different ways communities try to handle the problems. The disregard that we have as humans for nature around us, and what we do may have a much larger impact than we are aware of.
   - Much, much more engaged in this situation and more willing to learn. Very interesting method of teaching here!

2. *What questions or puzzles remain?*
   - If this problem were real, would my thought pattern have been the same? How many more problems come from one seemingly simple problem?

5

HOW DO YOU DESIGN A PROBLEM-BASED LEARNING CURRICULUM?

NOW THAT YOU HAVE A SENSE OF HOW THE EVENTS OF PBL play themselves out in classrooms, we'll step back and consider the design (Chapter 5) and implementation (Chapter 6) which, of course, precede the planning for instruction represented by our model for PBL.

In any design activity, we need to be clear about the essential elements that are available to us. What's on our palette? A friend who is a successful landscape designer sees plant materials as representing varying colors, textures, and forms. These then are the components she blends into a coherent design, varying one or more, but always conscious of the interplay and balance among the three in the overall plan. As we design PBL experiences, we must be aware of three essential elements—context, students, and curriculum—and the interrelationship among the three that contributes to coherent, holistic learning experiences. Where do we begin?

Thinking About Context

Many times in curriculum design and development we start with the knowledge, skills, and dispositions we believe our students should know, be able to do, and value. Through task analysis and from our experience, we piece together what we consider to be a holistic and connected lesson or unit. In doing so, we often miss the relationships and connections that provide coherence and relevance for our students who must engage with the learning experience. For example, in designing a unit around tropical rain forests, beginning with the flora and fauna and leading up to their impact upon global environmental issues, we might overlook connections to the local culture, the economic development of the region, or society's role in their destruction. As educators, we tend to assume students will "see" complex interrelationships when, for the most part, they don't.

In designing a problem-based learning experience, we begin instead with the problematic situation—a fully integrated whole—and tease out the knowledge, skills, and dispositions that are exposed by the authentic context of the problem. Many times we have heard Grant Wiggins speak of "content as the means to performance ends" as he points out the need for evidence of understanding. PBL experiences expose rich content and skills and place students in situations where they can interact with both the people and products authentic to that situation. Students go beyond knowing to understanding as they move across contexts and situations, adapting, coping, and thinking deeply. "That's why PBL is such an elegant piece of design" (Wiggins and Jacobs 1995).

Thinking About Students

As we design in-context curriculum, we are compelled to carefully consider students' learning characteristics and interests. What makes students unique as a group or as individuals? We encourage you to make a list of your learners' characteristics and add to it periodically. One middle grade teacher began by thinking about her students' knowledge, skills, developmental level, and dispositions, and generated the following list:

- Want to be independent—yet can be childlike and develop hero worship.
- Criticize society.
- Are ready to refine reasoning skills and understand abstract concepts.
- Can be self-conscious about new tasks.
- Care deeply about their personal situation and want to fit in with peer group.

A high school teacher at an alternative school began with this list:

- Rebel against the traditional teaching methods.
- Perceive school as an alternative to prison.
- Have experienced a large measure of failure.
- Cannot see a practical application for what is taught in school.
- Value real experiences.

Thinking About Curriculum

Before designing a PBL experience, we need to develop a set of priorities for our teaching. Consider the outcomes for any unit or course. What are some conceptual, skill-based, and dispositional outcomes that you and your school value highly enough to invest instructional time in? One middle grade teacher prepared this list:

- Understand such issues as biodiversity and economic impacts.
- Design and conduct experiments.
- Use graphs to illustrate probability and interpret data.
- Communicate effectively with a given audience.
- Develop self-directed learning strategies.
- Appreciate the views and contributions of others.

A high school teacher in an integrated health occupations program included the following outcomes:

- Culture and identify microorganisms.
- Differentiate between "normal" and "diseased" human body states.
- Describe how a catalyst affects a rate of reaction.
- Explore several methods of chemical analysis.
- Develop library skills.
- Use the Internet as a research source.

By explicitly exposing what we already know about the essential elements of context, students, and curriculum, we are better able to blend and balance their contribution to each element of the design of PBL curriculum as it begins to meld into implementation and unfold naturally.

We see most effective PBL units unfolding quite naturally through the design component and the decisions teacher-designers make as they choose a relevant problem of worth, develop the unit around this problem, and build their teaching and learning template. Teacher-coaches then implement their plans through a coaching strategy as students meet, investigate, and attempt to resolve their ill-structured problem. Figure 5.1 (an expansion of Figure 2.2) presents our conception of the flow of a PBL unit from idea to actuality.

Generating and Playing with Ideas

Increasingly, teachers are confronted with the challenge of providing sufficient coverage. On the one hand, there is an increasing volume of curriculum to cover; on the other, there is a call to cover the curriculum in more depth. One way to deal with this problem is to shift our perspective and play with ideas. Play may not be what you normally think of when organizing curriculum and planning for instruction. But play, intellectual play, enables us to deal with the new ideas, consider what's possible, and identify what's missing (Doll 1993).

Recently, we worked with a cadre of 16 Illinois educators whose goals centered around integrating PBL and the scientific literacy habits of mind identified by the Illinois State Board of Education (Illinois State Board of Education's Center for Scientific Literacy 1994). These habits of mind are summarized in Figure 5.2 (see p. 48).

FIGURE 5.1
The Flow of a PBL Unit

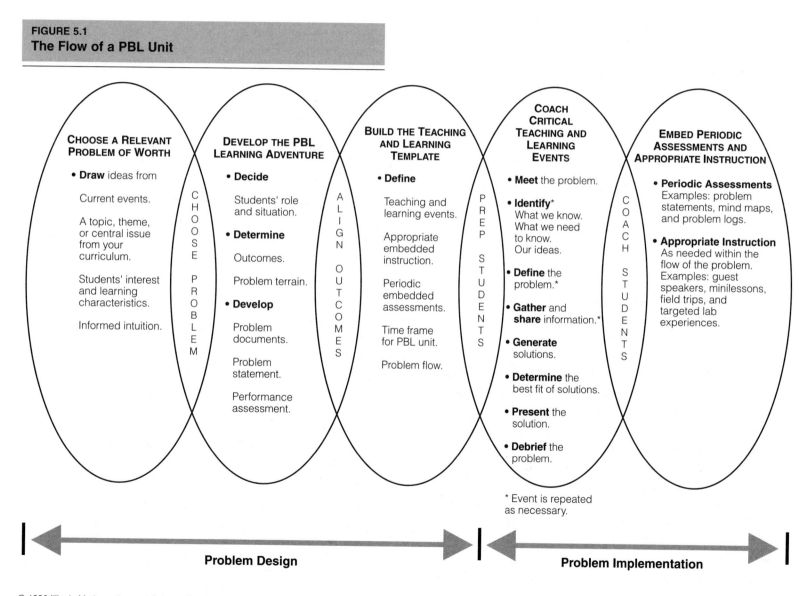

CHOOSE A RELEVANT PROBLEM OF WORTH

- **Draw** ideas from

  Current events.

  A topic, theme, or central issue from your curriculum.

  Students' interest and learning characteristics.

  Informed intuition.

CHOOSE PROBLEM

DEVELOP THE PBL LEARNING ADVENTURE

- **Decide**

  Students' role and situation.

- **Determine**

  Outcomes.

  Problem terrain.

- **Develop**

  Problem documents.

  Problem statement.

  Performance assessment.

ALIGN OUTCOMES

BUILD THE TEACHING AND LEARNING TEMPLATE

- **Define**

  Teaching and learning events.

  Appropriate embedded instruction.

  Periodic embedded assessments.

  Time frame for PBL unit.

  Problem flow.

PREP STUDENTS

COACH CRITICAL TEACHING AND LEARNING EVENTS

- **Meet** the problem.

- **Identify***
  What we know.
  What we need to know.
  Our ideas.

- **Define** the problem.*

- **Gather** and **share** information.*

- **Generate** solutions.

- **Determine** the best fit of solutions.

- **Present** the solution.

- **Debrief** the problem.

COACH STUDENTS

EMBED PERIODIC ASSESSMENTS AND APPROPRIATE INSTRUCTION

- **Periodic Assessments**
  Examples: problem statements, mind maps, and problem logs.

- **Appropriate Instruction**
  As needed within the flow of the problem. Examples: guest speakers, minilessons, field trips, and targeted lab experiences.

* Event is repeated as necessary.

◄——————— **Problem Design** ———————►   ◄——————— **Problem Implementation** ———————►

FIGURE 5.2
Scientific Literacy Habits of Mind

A capacity to question, comprehend, interpret, and make inferences.

An ability to communicate mathematically and scientifically.

An awareness that the nature of science and mathematics is ongoing, evolving, and refined through investigation.

An appreciation of the interdependence and interrelatedness of science, mathematics, and technology.

An understanding of the strengths and limitations of science, mathematics, and technology in our complex world.

Source: Illinois State Board of Education's Center for Scientific Literacy 1994, p. 1.

We played with several idea "umbrellas" as we began the PBL design process to develop a program for middle grade students—with a goal of improving their scientific literacy. Here are the beginnings of messy, ill-structured problems. What opportunities do you see to cover several goals and ignite student interest under a single umbrella?

Building Another Bridge to Accommodate Increasing Traffic

The Fox Valley area is growing steadily. Traffic is increasing, and a new bridge across the Fox River is needed. Several sites have been proposed, but there is opposition to each. One site crosses a forest preserve that contains rare plant and animal species. Other sites concern homeowners who want the bridge built somewhere else. Is the bridge really needed? At which site should it be built? Who decides?

Underage Smoking in the Community

Underage smoking is on the rise in the school district. Beyond the obvious addiction problem and dangerous health risks to the children, additional concerns have surfaced. Cigarettes are a discipline problem in the middle school and a focus of rebellious behavior. Several students have turned to stealing to get money for cigarettes. What, if anything, should the middle school do about student smoking?

Declining Frog Populations in the County

The middle school backs up to wetlands that contain a wide variety of unusual and interesting plants and animals. This area has been used for years by the science classes to collect and study plants and animals. Lately, students and teachers have noticed that the frog population has decreased dramatically. It is now hard to find frogs at all. What happened to all the frogs?

Look to your community for current issues and consider opening some umbrellas of your own. Newspapers, weekly news magazines, talk radio, town council and park board meetings, and the Internet may help to seed your thinking.

Mapping the Terrain of Problem Possibilities

Working from a bank of possibilities like these umbrella ideas, visualize each topic in some way and map out the terrain of problem ideas and connections. An upper elementary teacher mapped out or webbed several other idea possibilities that interested her because of learner appeal, integrative curricular yield, and real-world connections. Figure 5.3 shows three map skeletons as she added topics and details related to her central ideas.

Mapping is an invaluable tool for multiple purposes in PBL. Figure 5.4 (see p. 51) details how we have used maps.

Once you can see and examine the terrain of these possibilities, look for areas of conflict or dissonance. What is unacceptable in each situation? What pulls you in, sparks a need-to-know, and begs for resolution? Are there multiple stakeholders who have a vested interest in this problem? One teacher contends that with messy, ill-structured problems, anything students come up with as a solution "is going to be controversial to one person or another. That's just part of problem solving." We look also for situations that have multiple solutions. Most problems—especially real-world problems—rarely have one right answer.

Select a problematic center for your PBL experience that maximizes both engagement and learning. Two middle school teachers, Louise and Karoline, grapple with the issues of motivation and curricular payoff in a brief question-and-answer interchange about restoring a prairie adjacent to their school:

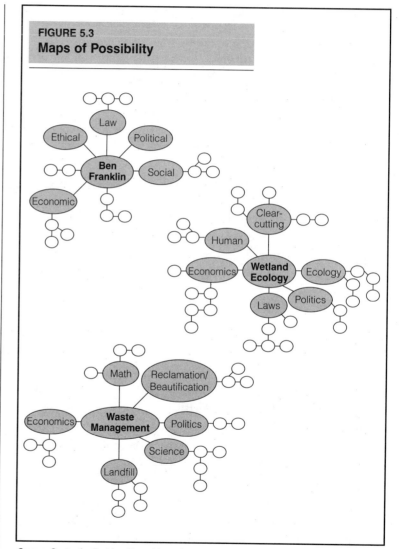

FIGURE 5.3
Maps of Possibility

Source: Center for Problem-Based Learning 1996a.

Louise: What is it we're actually trying to do? I mean, are we trying to get them to see—are we trying to get them to get the rest of the students to see how they can save prairies in general?

Karoline: But I think we also want them to make a connection. I mean they could learn all they want to about this prairie, but if . . . we don't get them to hook the rest of the school population into why we care about a prairie, then I think they are going to feel almost used.

They have chosen a problem that exposes rich content, but will their students care enough about saving and restoring the prairie adjacent to the school? And will students feel empowered to have meaningful input into the resolution? These connections are essential if learners are to delve into the complexity of the situation and move toward action.

Planning a Problem-Based Learning Adventure

More than one learner has commented that PBL is a learning adventure. With any journey, though, getting where you want to go requires planning and preparation. We're not talking about planning for instruction and the details of day-to-day implementation now (see Chapters 4 and 6), but rather the overall sense of knowing where you're going, how you're going to get there, and what you'll need to do once you've arrived. This work sounds much more linear than it really is; actually, these activities are so interrelated that they evolve together:

- Identify learning outcomes.
- Decide on a problematic situation and students' roles in that situation.
- Figure out how students will meet the problem.
- Develop the anticipated problem statement.
- Describe the performance of understanding.
- Gather information.

More and more, as we continue to design a PBL learning experience, we put ourselves in our learners' places and anticipate their questions, thinking, needs, and responses to the ambiguity and complexity of ill-structured problems. In this way, we begin to plan for their PBL learning adventure. Figure 5.5 (see p. 52) charts a course and identifies critical milestones in this planning process.

Knowing Where You're Going

Two important planning activities help frame the students' learning adventure:

- Identifying the learning outcomes exposed by the problem.
- Describing the performance of understanding in which learners will engage as an authentic companion to their investigation.

Identify Learning Outcomes. Once we have chosen the problematic topic to center our PBL experience around, we identify the learning outcomes to serve as our beacon during the running of the problem. Extending a map of possibility into a curriculum map is one way. By examining concepts, skills, and processes exposed through mapping, teachers make explicit connections to curriculum by adding to their maps direct curricular references at the perimeter. This connection is shown in Figure 5.6 (see p. 53) by a document shape with the upper right corner turned down. The figure is a curriculum map conceptualized by a team of teachers who developed PBL curriculum for IMSA's Summer Challenge Program for middle school students. These students, as consultants for a local mayor, were charged with determining the best possible location for a new municipal landfill. A problem such as this one exposes rich content in multiple subject areas.

A planning team for a different program, the Illinois Problem-Based Learning Network (IPBLN), chose to categorize and list learning outcomes exposed through the mapping process, as shown in Figure 5.7 (see p. 56). The outcomes are based on the major goals for their program related to content, self-directed learning, thinking and reasoning, and team collaboration (see Figure 5.8 on p. 57).

Describe the Performance of Understanding. What meaningful performance assessment will allow students to interact with the problem's real stakeholders and show what students have learned in an integrated and authentic way? To resolve this question, we encourage teachers to think carefully about the problem and select an assessment that is authentic to the situation. In reality, this decision is not something we can determine until we are clear about the role that students will take on as they immerse themselves in the problem.

FIGURE 5.4
Using Maps to Make Thinking Visible

Mind mapping is one way to record thinking visually so that it can be reviewed, organized, and refined. Several types can be used:

Maps of possibility. You can select and focus a problem by mapping the terrain of the topic and what you want a problem to accomplish.

Anticipated problem maps. You can map the actual components that present themselves in a given problem. These maps can help you plan for necessary resources by anticipating how students might make their way through a problem.

Curriculum maps. You can map the curricular connections within a given problem. These maps can help you identify key curricular outcomes for assessment and reporting.

Problem maps. Students can map the problem space to see the scope and connections within a problematic situation. These maps can help students generate ideas about needed resources or information and develop hypotheses about potential solutions.

Teachers can assess student learning by examining changes in students' actual maps of the problem throughout the teaching and learning process and by comparing students' final maps of the problem with maps generated by experts in the field of inquiry.

FIGURE 5.5
Planning a Problem-Based Learning Adventure

Before taking to the road, consider your destination and choose or define outcomes worthy of your effort, students' investment, and the curriculum.

How will students meet the messy situation that contains the problem needing resolution?

- How are the boundaries of the problem space determined?

- What alerts students to their **role** and **situation**?

- Is it a document, a drama, or ??

How will students make the journey?

- What **role** will capture students' interest and provide a platform for making a contribution to problem resolution?

- What messy **situation** will draw students into its depths without broadcasting the root problem, foreshadowing the solution, or providing too much information?

Remember . . .

Getting where you want to go requires planning and preparation!

How will students define the root problem?

- How will you create the scenario and organize the information so that students will get to the essential issue and critical conditions of the problem?

- Knowing what you know about your students and the problematic scenario, how do you think students will define the root problem?

How will students show that they have arrived at their destination?

What meaningful **performance assessment** will afford students the opportunity to interact with real stakeholders of this problem **and** show what they have learned in an integrated and authentic way?

FIGURE 5.6
Curriculum Map for the Landfill Problem

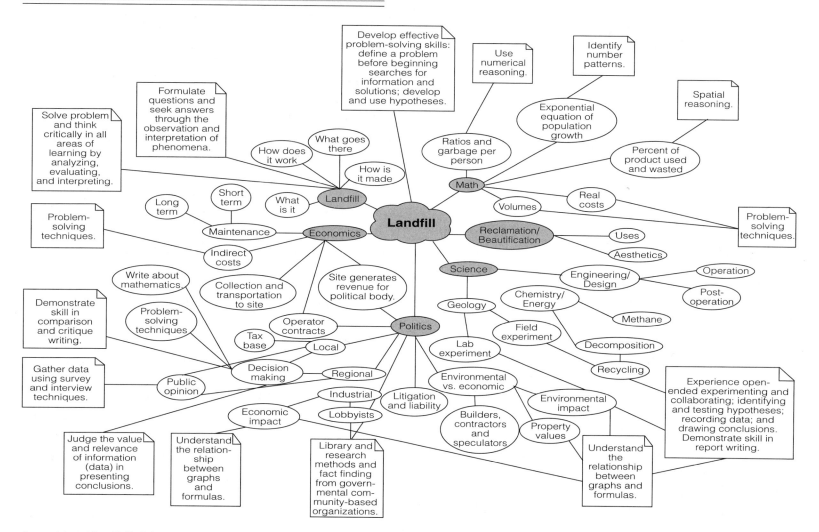

Source: Adapted from Finkle, Briggs, Hinton, Thompson, and Dods 1994.

Knowing How You're Going to Get There

Once you know where you are going, you'll need to consider how you and your students will travel through the twists and turns of the problem. We have found that before developing a more detailed teaching and learning template (see Chapter 4), it is essential that you carry out the following tasks:

- Decide on a problematic situation and the students' roles in that situation.
- Figure out how students will meet the problem.
- Develop the anticipated problem statement.
- Gather relevant information.

As we stated in the previous section, even though these actions are presented in a seemingly linear fashion, in reality, they evolve together. Gathering relevant information from experts or local contacts will more than likely inform the selection of a role and situation. The interrelatedness of these planning actions cannot be stressed enough.

Decide on a Problematic Situation and Students' Role in That Situation. As mentioned earlier, ill-structured problems present a challenge for many different stakeholders. If we examine the issue of landfill site selection in a suburban area (see earlier chapter discussion on site selection and Figure 5.6), we can identify many individuals who might have a vested interest in the problem and potential solutions—local politicians, homeowners whose property values are at risk, environmentalists, corporate officials of the landfill management group, taxpayers, department of transportation officials, soil and water district scientists, and so on.

Our challenge is to select a role in which the students will gain a full understanding of the problem and its complexity. We want them to consider the central issue and not simply address the concerns of one set of stakeholders. We also want them to step into a role that will interest them and provide them with a sense of empowerment in the situation. In the landfill problem as developed for upper middle school students, the designers placed students in the role of environmental engineers employed by a consulting firm. The firm had been hired to advise the mayor of a local community about the viability of three potential sites.

We need to stress the importance, once again, of playing with several possibilities. The choice of role and situation is critical in design. An upper elementary grade teacher tested a variety of possibilities before making her selection. Figure 5.9 (see p. 57) shows roles she was considering to engage students in the problem of wetlands development. In this problem, an oil company was seeking to purchase drilling rights within a protected wetland habitat for migrating birds.

Asking herself, "What if the central issue is . . . and the role is . . . and the final performance would logically be to . . . ?" she was able to select a role and situation appropriate for her students, where they would need to consider varying stakeholder positions. She then created an anticipated problem map that reflected her chosen role and situation and played out the problem as she thought students might (see Figure 5.10 on p. 59). Seeing the curricular richness exposed through mapping, she identified outcomes relevant for her 4th and 5th graders, adding such references to her map in the form of documents with a turned-down-corner.

You may wish to map out different possibilities for role and situation, highlighting, adding, and deleting concepts according to the demands of the role and situation with which you are working. You will see how problems can change significantly.

Another important consideration is the scope of the chosen role. If the focus of the problem and role is relatively narrow, the problem experience is more contained. For example, students may grapple with a problem that involves a personal relationship, an individual's decision-making struggle, or a problem involving the student and a peer group. If the focus of the problem and role, on the other hand, is more global and involves more stakeholders, it is more complex and deserves more time and other resources. These latter types of problems might engage students as legislators considering the passage of a particular bill, as stockholders assessing the merits of a merger or acquisition, or as members of the scientific community weighing the ethical issues related to the use or misuse of new and controversial technology. In defining these two extremes, we recognize the infinite possibilities that occupy the middle ground.

It is important to emphasize the value of roles within a problem inquiry. Roles situated within the problem scenario enable students and teachers alike to step outside the constraints of familiar roles and become coinvestigators in the problem inquiry. They can be scientists, homeowners, police—anyone.

Another benefit of roles is that they personalize learning and give students ownership of the problem. As stakeholders in the problem, students are immersed in the situation. They are situated in the center of the learning experience rather than on the perimeter. Dorothy Heathcote (Heathcote and Herbert 1980) contrasts these two perspectives as learning about things that are "here" or learning about things that are "there." "Here" is much more immediate and engaging, leading to deeper understanding. The student must take a stand on an issue, such as underage smoking, building a bridge, or planning a sanitary landfill.

That is not to say that students should always assume a role outside self. If the problematic situation is one in which students would naturally own the problem, then keeping their perspective and their natural empathic connection as students makes sense. In this type of situation, we also want to make sure that students have a voice in resolving the problem.

Several schools have used the problem of how to renovate a school or construct a new school. In most cases, students had an opportunity to present their recommendations to the school board, meet with the architect or building design team, and actually see some of their suggestions incorporated into the school's design. Giving students these opportunities assures that the PBL learning adventure transports them from empathy to advocacy and possible action (Newmann 1990).

FIGURE 5.7
Map of Possibility for the Tobacco Use Problem

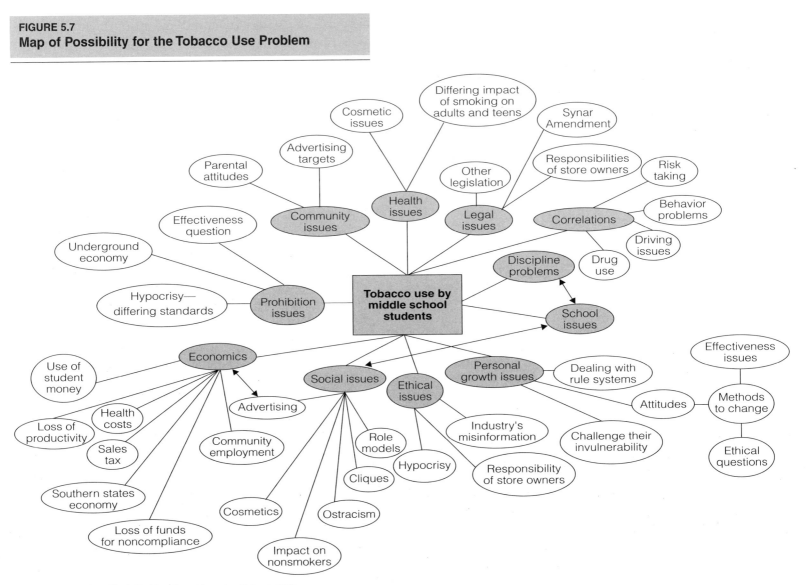

Source: Adapted from Illinois Problem-Based Learning Network 1996.

FIGURE 5.8
Learning Outcomes for the Tobacco Use Problem

Content

Examine tobacco use choices and consequences for teenagers.

Review legal and social issues related to tobacco use among teenagers.

Consider health, ethical, and economic issues involving tobacco.

Analyze sources of tobacco research and information.

Know background information about the tobacco industry.

Self-Directed Learning

Develop assertiveness skills.

Identify relevant and reliable materials.

Utilize effective communication skills.

Develop personal responsibility.

Make choices based on evidence.

Thinking and Reasoning

Generate questions that focus and direct inquiry.

Analyze data from multiple sources.

Read, interpret, and transform data from graphs and charts.

Compare and contrast varied perspectives.

Develop critical thinking and decision-making skills.

Synthesize information.

Team Collaboration

Engage in healthy interactions with peers, adults, and community.

Provide efficient and effective help and assistance to each other.

Exchange needed resources with team.

Encourage achievement of goals.

Source: Adapted from Illinois Problem-Based Learning Network 1996.

FIGURE 5.9
Testing Role Possibilities for the Wetlands Problem

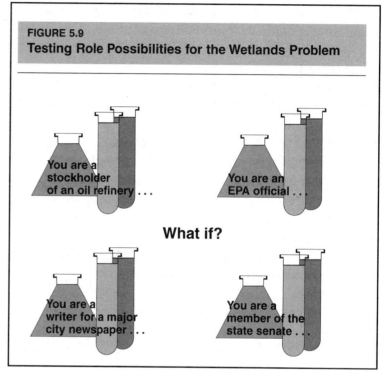

Source: Adapted from Vitale-Ortlund 1994.

Figure Out How Students Will Meet the Problem.
How will students meet the messy situation that contains the root problem needing resolution? Is it a document, a phone message, a video clip, or a drama? Are these artifacts authentic or simulated? Remember the TV series, "Mission Impossible"? Jim and the team listened to a short audiotape overviewing the situation and reviewed a dossier of pertinent materials.

Many teachers are surprised at the power of authentic-looking documents as hooks to capture student interest and frame the PBL adventure. To continue with the landfill site selection example cited earlier in the chapter, students received simulated letters from varying stakeholders in the problem. A letter like the one shown in Figure 5.11 (see p. 60), coupled with the staging of a staff meeting between Dr. Pace's representative (the teacher-coach) and her staff of environmental engineers (the students), serves to engage students and initiate their problem inquiry.

A first-rate introduction to a problem gives learners a sense of their stake and role in the problem and just enough information to launch their inquiry. Too much information may kill the desire to know more; too little can shut down the learners' attempts to get started.

Develop the Anticipated Problem Statement. Picture the circus performer who balances plates on the tips of reeds and spins them, trying to get as many as possible spinning at once. In designing a problem, there are times when we, too, need to keep a few plates spinning, such as when we are determining the problematic situation, students' role, and problem engagement. Although these design features are presented here linearly, they are really defined and refined in concert. Given the stakeholder role and problematic situation you decide upon, as well as how the students meet the problematic scenario, you'll need to anticipate what the students might identify as the real or root problem. In other words, as designer, you anticipate the stakeholder's perspective and context.

Your anticipated problem statement is the key feature to help you shape the design elements into a coherent plan for instruction. All the teacher's planning and all the students' learning are focused and guided by a clear statement of the problem. From our experience, these statements have two essential parts:

- A statement of the central issue of the problem.
- The identification of conditions that will signal an acceptable solution.

We often use the following guide or heuristic to frame our problem statements:

How can we . . .	[state the issue] . . .
so that . . .	[state the conditions].

Example:

How can we . . .	come to a decision about ownership of the wetlands . . .
so that . . .	we address

- Jobs of refinery workers.
- Revenue to the state.
- Ecology of the wetlands.
- Clear cutting of the wetlands.
- Law protecting the wetlands.
- Political pressure.
- Political votes.
- Political jobs.

FIGURE 5.10
Anticipated Problem Map for the Wetlands Problem

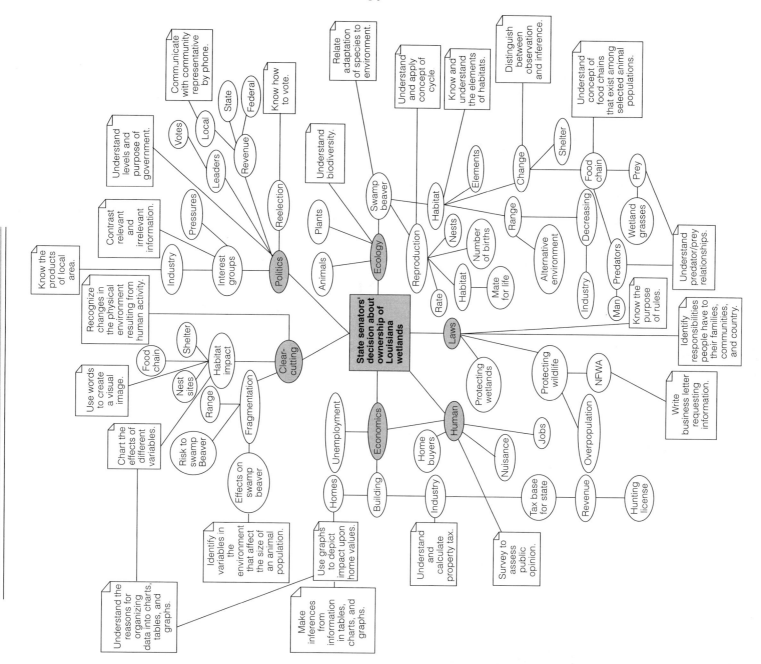

Source: Adapted from Vitale-Ortlund 1994.

Remember, this anticipated problem statement is a design tool—not something we provide for the students. They must define the real problem for themselves. It may take several refinement cycles, but this struggle to grasp the whole of the situation is essential. We want to engage our learners in the messiness of the situation so that they experience the tentativeness, incompleteness, and the desire to know more before they attempt to craft a solution.

Einstein once remarked that both the most difficult and the most critical part of problem solving is problem definition. The easiest way to begin would be to "give" students their problem, but if you did that, you would also take away the opportunity for students to develop important problem-sensing skills and inhibit their creativity, value building, and engagement. Defining the problem for students reinforces the notion that the task of problem solving is quick and easy: Follow the rules, march to conclusion, and justify it. Often students identify issues and conditions that never occurred to the teacher.

Gather Information. As we plan PBL units, we usually gather an abundance of information from the community, the library, the Internet, and available experts. It is important to note that the students should only be given basic information on the problem and the larger questions to be resolved. This information may be in the form of a letter or a newspaper clipping. For one biomedical problem where students were in a role as consulting physicians, they received a phone message slip alerting them to a consultation appointment in two weeks (really their performance

---

FIGURE 5.11
Meet the Problem: Letter for the Landfill Problem

Village of Gotham
22 South First Street
Gotham, IL 60134   Walter R. Powers, Mayor

October 3, 1997

Dr. Michele Barron Pace
Prairie Environmental Services
1500 West Sullivan Road
Aurora, IL 60506-1000

Dear Dr. Pace:

This letter is to notify you that the Village of Gotham wishes to contract the services of your company to determine the feasibility of utilizing one of the available sites for a new landfill. This site is to replace our current Settler's Hill site, which is rapidly approaching capacity.

The sites, all owned by Cane County and therefore immediately available, are identified on the enclosed map as Gotham East, Gotham West, and Nelson Lake West.

I believe all other aspects of our solid waste disposal plan are effective and operating successfully.

Sincerely,

Walter R. Powers, Mayor

Source: Adapted from Finkle, Briggs, Hinton, Thompson, and Dods 1994.

assessment), a radiologist's report, and the social worker's field notes on the patient. Once students identify what the root problem is and what they need to know, they will gather the necessary information from multiple sources. At this time, you may choose to satisfy some of their identified needs—or not.

Knowing What You'll Need to Do Once You've Arrived

We have now come full circle to a question posed earlier: What meaningful performance assessment will allow students to interact with the problem's real stakeholders and show what they have learned in an integrated and authentic way? Now that we are clear about the role or stakeholder position that students will take on as they immerse themselves in the problematic situation *and* we have anticipated the root problem they will identify, we can decide how they will bring their inquiry to a close. We want the final performance to provide an opportunity for authentic assessment of learners' thinking and actions in their role and circumstances, making a direct connection between the habits of mind nurtured in the classroom and those needed in the real world.

Over and over again, we have witnessed students rise to the occasion and outperform their teacher's grandest expectations. We have also seen the reverse—where student interest and enthusiasm for the problem inquiry flags as the inquiry winds down. What makes the difference between these two very different outcomes? *Learners want to know that their efforts will have consequences.* If they believe that someone will think about and value their work, they are

more likely to undertake that work with enthusiasm and rigor.

Throughout the inquiry, students place themselves in the middle of the problem investigation. They interact authentically with the information, problem, and players. They own the problem and anticipate having some influence upon its resolution or at the very least a similar problem. Designing a performance assessment where students are confronted by or presented to real stakeholders raises the stakes considerably. Questions and challenges posed by those who have actually lived the problem usually get at deeper levels of understanding and knowing, exposing the problem's rough edges. Staging the performance so that it mirrors how actual stakeholders might interact adds another measure of relevance. Figure 5.12 (see p. 62) shows examples of performance scenarios based on specific roles.

It's Worth the Effort!

After a proposed policy was presented to a mock school board, one middle school student wrote this comment in a reflective journal entry:

> I'm a straight A student, but it's mostly because I know how to find answers in the textbooks. I've never had to defend my own answers—I think this is the first time I've ever had to think! COOL . . .

In a journal entry written earlier, when students were considering possible solutions, here is what one of her peers wrote:

It seems like when other teachers know our ideas are stupid, the ideas are dismissed. The teachers never say the idea is stupid, but the way the ideas get dismissed lets us know we came up with a stupid idea. The way you [PBL teacher] . . . asked questions made us go all the way through our own thoughts. If it turned out the idea was stupid, it's because we figured it out ourselves.

Here is what their PBL teacher wrote:

There was no way I could have predicted that adolescents would be able to intellectualize the problem as clearly as they did. It was my contention that they wouldn't understand the larger problem present, didn't understand a school system's hierarchy, and shouldn't have input into decision making. However, the teens . . . happily disproved my predictions! . . . I guess I have to say those kids have jolted me back into the reality that just because they're kids doesn't mean they have to be babied!

Summary

The common threads woven through all the elements of design—context, students, and curriculum—enable us to design coherent PBL learning experiences. Healthy measures of openness and playfulness enable us to step outside familiar structures and see the relevant problems that reside in holistic real-world experiences.

Once you know the scope of your PBL adventure—where you're going, how you're going to get there, and what you'll need know when you've arrived—you're ready to consider PBL implementation. Chapter 6 discusses new roles for teachers and students in PBL classrooms, then helps you consider the question: *Why, how, and what do I coach?*

FIGURE 5.12
Designing Authentic Performance Scenarios

Role or Perspective	Situation or Expectation	Performance Scenario
Environmental engineer	Advise city mayor.	Prepare proposal or white paper.
Citizen's focus group	Advise county agency.	Develop action plan.
Congressional staffer	Investigate viability of legislation.	Testify before a House subcommittee hearing.
Physician	Question a diagnosis.	Conduct a patient consultation.
City emergency worker	Prepare for unprecedented floods.	Design an emergency information pamphlet.
Student interest group	Challenge proposed action limiting access, rights, or privileges.	Make a presentation at a school board meeting.

6

How Do You Implement Problem-Based Learning?

ONCE YOU HAVE DESIGNED A PROBLEM YOU BELIEVE HAS worth and will engage your students, you are ready to begin implementing it. We explore implementing PBL in your classroom in this chapter.

Problem-based learning is one of a range of constructivist strategies for teaching and learning, based on philosophical positions we presented in earlier chapters. We suggest that a helpful analogy for the work of teachers in PBL is the work of athletic coaches. Coaches typically work on the sidelines, supporting players in decision making and strategy selection. Because this analogy helps many people understand a teacher's role in PBL, we call teachers' work "coaching."

We have found that for most teachers beginning to explore PBL, becoming comfortable teaching within this role of coach is a profound learning experience. "How do I interact with my students? How do I manage this complex process? What kinds of things will my students and I be doing in PBL?" In this chapter, we consider coaching in PBL.

New Roles for Teachers and Students

Again and again, PBL teachers with whom we have worked speak eloquently about the challenges inherent in rethinking their entire conception of teaching and learning (Sage and Torp 1997). Students, too—particularly those who have been successful in a more traditional teaching setting—often struggle with their new role as active thinkers and learners and the higher degree of ambiguity they encounter in ill-structured problems. Also, as Figure 6.1 shows, these roles evolve gradually. Students, over time, take more responsibility for learning as they develop a set of skills and habits of mind for becoming more self-directed. Teachers, over time, need to provide different kinds of supports for student learning, but they never become unnecessary. Coaching is a highly active role for teachers. As teacher comments show, learning to guide involves trusting in PBL and redefining control:

> I think I'm realizing more and more that fear was my major obstacle to begin with, and that the more I trust, the better I become as a PBL teacher. What I was afraid of was that my students might not come through when the responsibility was in their hands for defining problem statements, for coming up with solution options, and what steps to take to pursue their solution options. I think that fear limited me in my coaching through my first year of trying PBL. This year I was able to pull back on that a little and hand the ball to them. The more I trust them, the more successful it is. I do much less limiting of students' options and thinking when I trust them in that way.
>
> —Mary Biddle, Social Studies Teacher
> Franklin Middle School, Champaign, Ill.

> It's the old control issue; you can't really control the journey, but you can help guide. We can decide what to do as facilitators—whether we need embedded instruction or something else.
>
> —Louise Robb, Language Arts Teacher
> Barrington Middle School, Prairie Campus
> Barrington, Ill.

> Being a guide was the hardest thing for us to learn to do—finding a balance between what students need to know now, so I need to teach a lesson about that, and letting them go explore and maybe get a little frustrated and come back and work with their information. The other thing we learned was to be in the role of a questioner instead of a teller, to ask good questions that lead them down the role of thinking: "How are you thinking about this? What evidence do you have for that? Have you thought of another point of view?" If we focused on the thinking questions, the content we wanted them to learn came out; they were able to find it.
>
> —Laurie Friedrich, Staff Development Coordinator
> West High School, Wauwatosa, Wisc.

In this chapter, we use a particular problem experience to draw you into the process of coaching in PBL. The experience was used in John Thompson's ecology class at IMSA:

Role and Situation

Wolf populations are increasing in Minnesota and within a few years may no longer be protected under the federal Endangered Species Act. As a member of the Committee on the Environment and Natural Resources in the Minnesota House of

FIGURE 6.1
The Evolving Roles in PBL

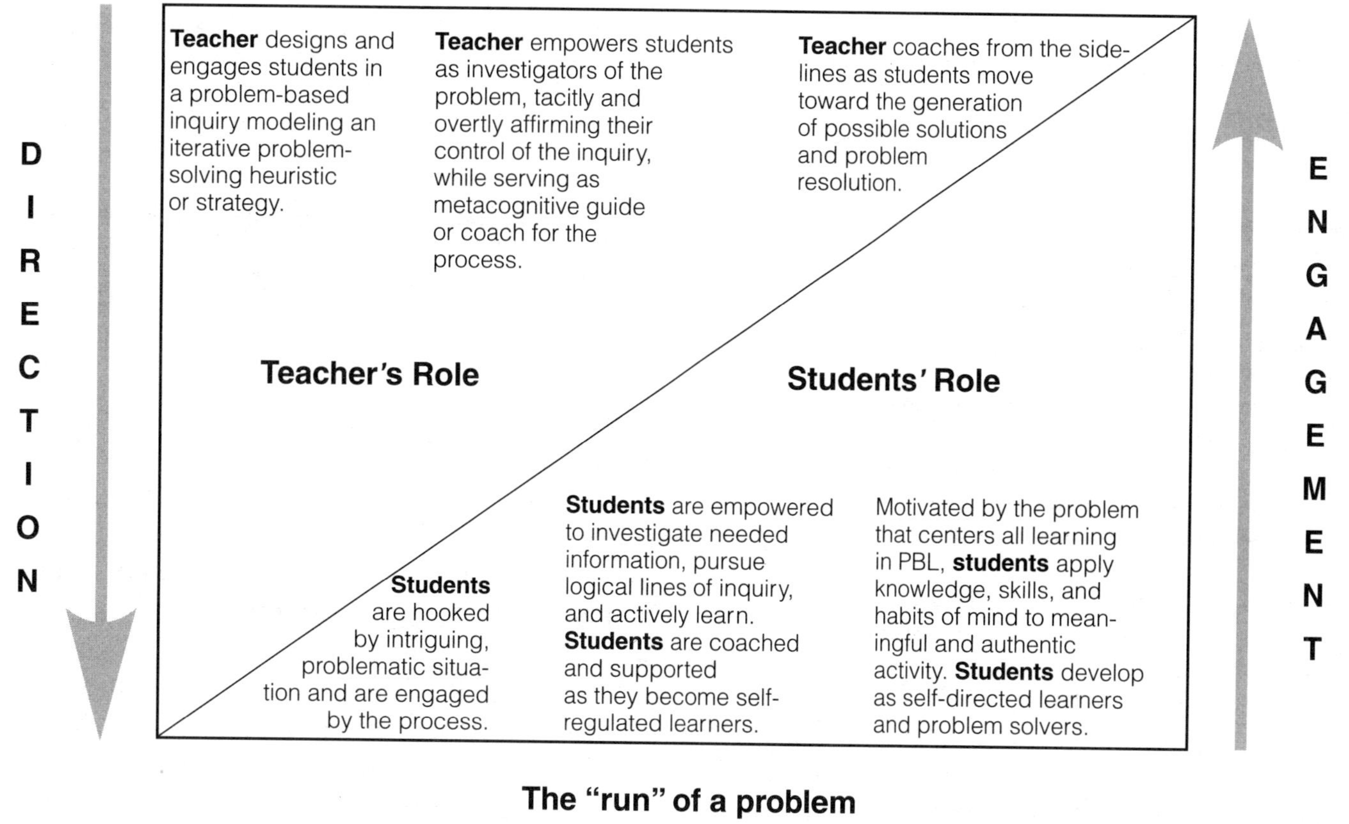

D I R E C T I O N

E N G A G E M E N T

Teacher designs and engages students in a problem-based inquiry modeling an iterative problem-solving heuristic or strategy.

Teacher empowers students as investigators of the problem, tacitly and overtly affirming their control of the inquiry, while serving as metacognitive guide or coach for the process.

Teacher coaches from the side-lines as students move toward the generation of possible solutions and problem resolution.

Teacher's Role

Students' Role

Students are empowered to investigate needed information, pursue logical lines of inquiry, and actively learn. **Students** are coached and supported as they become self-regulated learners.

Motivated by the problem that centers all learning in PBL, **students** apply knowledge, skills, and habits of mind to meaningful and authentic activity. **Students** develop as self-directed learners and problem solvers.

Students are hooked by intriguing, problematic situation and are engaged by the process.

The "run" of a problem

Representatives, how would you explain your support for a newly proposed state wolf management plan to a group of your expert constituents?

The students, in role as state legislators, are presented with an actual piece of proposed legislation, Minnesota House Bill #1891, and have about 15 days to prepare for discussing it with a panel of experts.

What Is Coaching?

I think you make decisions about content. Is this something that is on the fringe that the students can be held responsible for because they missed it? Or is it a real central chord to where the problem is going? If so, then through coaching questions or some kind of dialogue I would ask enough for them to bring it up.
—John Thompson, Science/Biology Teacher
Illinois Mathematics and Science Academy, Aurora, Ill.

The teacher in North American schools is faced with a mind-boggling array of mutually incompatible expectations and imperatives. . . . The practice of teaching is complex, uncertain, and dilemma-riddled.
—Clark 1988, p. 10

Both Thompson and Clark point out the complexity and constant stream of decision making inherent in any type of teaching, including coaching. As PBL teachers, we coach students' thinking; their communication, including the gathering and sharing of information; their group

process; and their problem-solving strategies. Our role shifts from one of *control* of what and how students learn to one of *mediation* of student learning. This coaching role requires us to be as engaged in learning as our students and to develop a sense of flow in our teaching beliefs, actions, and decisions. Such work may initially cause some uneasiness, as Thompson's comments show:

I remember the first time I ran a problem—I kind of kept my fingers crossed under the desk the whole time, wondering if it was going to work. Now I've seen it work, and probably I'm more demanding in terms of the students, making them more responsible for their own research and learning.

In PBL, coaching is a process of goal setting, modeling, guiding, facilitating, monitoring, and providing feedback to students to support their active and self-directed thinking and learning. Teachers accomplish these goals by encouraging as much active learning as possible and by finding ways to make students' thinking visible.

Teacher John Thompson provides an example of what he does for the wolf problem:
They've heard the term "carrying capacity" now, but they don't know that the carrying capacity has been calculated at 2,000 wolves. So once they figure that out, my next questions would be: "Okay, now that we're 400 over, what does that mean, and how did the person you talked with figure out 2,000

was a capacity in the first place?" Well, that gets into some serious biology they wouldn't have gotten to if it had just been a point in some lecture. Now population dynamics have to be actively understood and applied to the situation.

To help accomplish these goals, Thompson assumes a supporting but still active sideline role (coach), offering help as needed and providing guidance as students (players) think, test strategies, and consider solutions. The big decision in each teaching moment, then, is deciding when to let the players play and when and how to intervene. As Liz Pine, a former student recalls, John Thompson decided to "let her play":

We had a hearing where we brought in some people, and we had to stand up and defend the position we'd taken. I was speaking for a group who'd been working on one portion of the research. At the end, this man said, "Have you considered how your wolf plan will affect the Native American populations in the region? They fall under different laws because of their religious practices and beliefs."

And I said, "I didn't have a clue!" We completely missed this aspect, because we were focusing somewhere else. That taught me to be a lot more thorough in research we're doing and to get different perspectives.

—Elizabeth Pine, Former IMSA Student, Ph.D. Student at University of California, Berkeley

In the next example, Thompson describes how he intervened using a deliberate instructional event to make sure students encountered important ecology content in this problem:

Hunting is the weak issue now; it's just coming slower than I would have thought. Now it's time to bring it in. Fortunately, I've done the preparation and gotten all the props so we can do something that will look realistic and infuse a little drama into the problem. So what the students are going to get is a phone call from a hunter who asks them to go out and look at this kill site on Tuesday. When they look at the kill site, the object is to understand that this is an animal severely weakened by arthritis, and that wolves kill the most vulnerable, but that hunting doesn't focus on the same segment of the population.

How and What Do I Coach?

The following is an excerpt from a conversation between Thompson and one of his students, Chris. It occurred just after Chris and two classmates, trying to get more information about what Minnesota counties would be affected by House Bill #1891, got off the phone with an expert from the International Wolf Center:

Chris: She's never heard of the bill. . . . It sounded like the only way we're really going to find out the actual information we need is by talking to the author of the bill.

Mr. Thompson: Well, let's go back. Be more specific; tell me exactly what you're trying to find out, plus what you've already learned from this phone conversation (facilitating student understanding through *diagnosing and questioning*).

Chris: We're looking for the counties that are going to have wolves introduced.

Mr. Thompson: Okay. Did you ask her where wolves are currently found? (*questioning*) You said something about the carrying capacity is exceeded.

Chris: Yeah, that's what she said.

Mr. Thompson: Did you get a number on the carrying capacity? (*questioning*)

Chris: No.

Mr. Thompson: Okay. So what you've got are bits and pieces of information. The question is, how do you begin to connect these? I would collectively (*modeling*)—the three of you—say: "What did I find out in this phone call? What do I know from the bill?" (*questioning*) And, "What's my next 'need to know'?" So when we go back upstairs (*managing group work*), you can say, "Look, I've just found out this and this, but it brings up a new set of questions like, I don't know what the carrying capacity is. . . ."

Chris: She was very curious about the bill.

Mr. Thompson: I'd imagine so. But look at the point. You're now talking to a real person who is curious about what you're doing. All of a sudden you're informing the real people instead of the real people informing you. That puts you in a pretty knowledgeable position (*using role and drama*) . . . . So while we can feel good about ourselves on that one, let's look at what the next level of questions is. She told us this. What are the implications? (*mentoring*)

As this coaching episode helps illustrate, and as we have learned from our experiences and observing others, *how* and *what* we coach breaks down into two broad processes:

- Exposing and facilitating student thinking and getting at deeper levels of understanding—through *diagnosing, mentoring, questioning,* and *modeling.*
- Managing the PBL process itself in your classroom—*adapting the PBL process, using role and drama, managing group work,* and *monitoring student engagement.*

These two processes are made possible by ongoing coaching, as well as by instruction and assessments *embedded* in the PBL process (see Figure 6.2 on p. 70).

Facilitating Student Understanding

Teachers of problem-based learning must coach students' thinking, inquiry, and metacognition as students work to solve problems. This process has several parts: diagnosing, mentoring, questioning, and modeling.

Diagnosing. One important role coaches must play in facilitating student understanding is educational diagnosis (Barrows 1988). The coach must identify students' learning needs and their level of engagement, so that students don't slide through a PBL experience without ever understanding the problem and its solution. Coaches observe students, listen to what they are saying (and not saying), carefully look at assessments embedded in the PBL experience, and *ask questions.*

Another format for diagnosis is asking students to map or web their current understanding of the problem, as teacher John Thompson did early in the PBL experience. Individual students may be struggling with reasoning, locating appropriate information, understanding concepts discussed by the group, or understanding the nature of the problem itself. Coaches can intervene with personal assistance or through encouraging the student's group to provide assistance. We suggest using focused, metacognitive questions, such as, "Were you able to find all the resources you wanted?" or "Does the way you have put that together make sense to you?" to challenge students in particular areas of difficulty.

We want to make very clear that we don't believe *teaching* is a dirty word (Harris and Graham 1996) in our model of PBL coaching. Successful PBL coaches diagnose students' learning needs and then arrange whatever support students need. Even direct instruction may be appropriately embedded when students need to know some background or facts or to learn a particular skill. For example, the day students made the phone call outlined in the conversation between Chris and Thompson, Thompson discovered that a number of his students didn't understand how to use long-distance information services. He led a brief, focused discussion on how to do that before students dispersed to place their various calls.

Mentoring. Another important part of facilitating student understanding is the coach's role as mentor to students (Duffy and Savery 1995). PBL coaches (mentors) seek out and value their students' (protégés) points of view. The coach does not take over thinking for students by telling them what to do or how to think, but does challenge them by inquiring at the leading edge of their thinking. The mentor and the protégés are learners together; the mentor helps students build bridges from their present understanding to new, more complex understandings (Brooks and Brooks 1993). The coach as mentor must also maintain appropriate levels of challenge during the PBL experience, prompting students to move further in their thinking but not push so hard that students become frustrated and give up.

One way Thompson and other coaches mentor students is to assign entries in student thinking logs. He may ask a focused question like, "What is your current understanding of predators?" and read and respond to student responses. Such logs can be used not only as measures of student thinking and possible frustration levels, but also as assess-

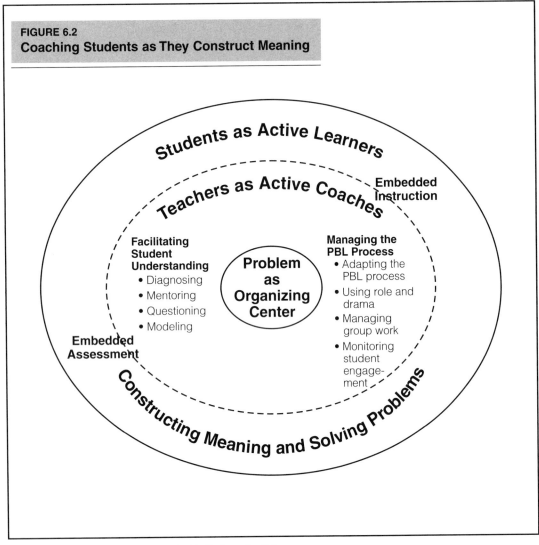

FIGURE 6.2
Coaching Students as They Construct Meaning

Students as Active Learners

Teachers as Active Coaches

Embedded
Instruction

**Facilitating
Student
Understanding**
• Diagnosing
• Mentoring
• Questioning
• Modeling

**Problem
as
Organizing
Center**

**Managing the
PBL Process**
• Adapting the
  PBL process
• Using role and
  drama
• Managing
  group work
• Monitoring
  student
  engage-
  ment

Embedded
Assessment

Constructing Meaning and Solving Problems

Note: Instruction and assessment are embedded in the entire PBL process.

ments embedded throughout a PBL experience.

Questioning. To facilitate student understanding, coaches must hold students to strict benchmarks of good thinking and reasoning, including specificity, defensibility, examination of bias, and consideration of opposing views. Probably the best way teachers can do this work is by questioning. Well-placed questions that probe students to think further or challenge them to reconsider their thinking not only help students consider different aspects of the problem situation, but also encourage them to become critical thinkers. Questions may also serve to redirect students or prompt them to set goals for their own inquiry.

We find Karen Kitchener's (1983) three-level model of cognitive processing, shown in Figure 6.3, is a helpful structure for considering questioning in an ill-structured problem experience:

- Cognition
- Metacognition
- Epistemic cognition

At the *cognitive* level, students compute, read, perceive, and comprehend information. *Metacognitive* questions help students monitor their own thinking process and consider appropriate strategies. *Epistemic cognition* refers to individuals' understanding of the nature of problems and includes knowledge about the limits and certainty of knowing, and the criteria for knowing. Figure 6.4 (see p. 72) gives general guidelines for questioning as PBL coaches.

Modeling. A fourth way coaches facilitate student understanding is by modeling the kinds of thinking behaviors they want their students to exhibit. Coaches may model openness to complexity and ambiguity, and willingness to engage in ambiguous situations. They may also model patience, particularly when listening to others and being open to what others are saying. As coaches, we should talk about and model our thinking and problem solving, not dispense information. We can also model metacognition through examples of our own thinking strengths and weaknesses, and what we have learned from solving problems. Perhaps most important is to model respecting the ideas and opinions of others through acknowledging the students' perspectives, as the coach models a willingness and ability to be a learner along with students.

Managing the PBL Process

A second major emphasis for coaches is managing the implementation of PBL in their particular classrooms. This management includes adapting the PBL process, using role

---

FIGURE 6.3
Three Levels of Thinking and Questioning

Level 1: Cognition (Thinking)	Level 2: Metacognition (Learning about thinking)	Level 3: Epistemic Cognition (Nature of knowing in ill-structured problems)
Questions coaches might ask:	*Questions coaches might ask:*	*Questions coaches might ask:*
What have you learned?	What, if anything, about your goals and strategies needs to change?	How do you know?
Are you sure?		What can we know? To what degree of certainty?
What seems important here?	What kinds of resources have been most helpful to you so far?	
What does this mean for our problem?		What is at stake?
	Have you considered _____? (process or strategy)	What solution fits best with the criteria in our problem statement?
Do you have enough facts to suggest _____?		

Source: Adapted from Kitchener 1983.

and drama, managing group work, and monitoring student engagement.

Adapting the PBL Process. The template of teaching and learning events we presented in Chapter 4 is a suggested structure for implementing PBL, not a rigid prescription for how PBL must be implemented. We highlight essential elements of PBL in Chapter 2, with the most important parameter being centering learning around an ill-structured problem. Beyond those parameters, the template of events can be flexible for use with many different students. Some coaches, for example, choose to have students develop a problem statement *before* the students identify what they know and need to know. These coaches believe defining the nature of the problem first helps keep the "knows" and "need to knows" more focused.

Many coaches work with the whole class on the know/need to know and problem statement events. Others, like teacher John Thompson during the wolf problem, choose to have students work in small groups to develop their own "know" and "need-to-know" lists before the class comes together as a whole. One reason for Thompson's decision was a high number of introverted students in the ecology class who felt more comfortable sharing in small groups than in the whole class setting. He also chose to wait until several days into the problem experience before developing problem statements, because he felt the problem statements would be too vague to be helpful until the students had gathered some information about the proposed bill. Students then individually mapped their under-

---

FIGURE 6.4
Guidelines for Questioning as PBL Coaches

Actively listen to what students are *and* are not saying.

Ask questions that require a rich response.

Use all three levels of cognitive questioning.

Avoid yes-or-no questions and one-word answers.

Pause to allow thoughtful responses.

Encourage and allow the conversation to reside among students as much as possible.

Avoid the temptation to correct immediately or interrupt.

Encourage support and justification of ideas—probe to extend student thinking.

Challenge data, assumptions, and sources.

Avoid feedback that cues students to the "rightness" of their statements; probe students frequently so probing is not viewed only as a cue for "wrongness."

---

standing of the problem. Figures 6.5 and 6.6 (see pp. 73, 74, respectively) are maps that represent one student's growing understanding and knowledge base about the problem.

Using Role and Drama. Frequently in a problem, coaches engage students by having them take on a role that might be unfamiliar to them (refer to Chapter 5 for more detail on role playing). The key to role playing is to learn to suspend disbelief to "get into the role" (Center for Problem-Based Learning 1996b). As the coach, you will help move students to a level of role playing that intimately involves them in the problem as insiders, so students own the problem and have more investment in solving it. Coaches are instrumental in preparing students for their roles by discussing role playing and often by providing props and scenery that help students manage their roles.

In the wolf problem, where students took on the role of state legislators, Thompson prepared students the day before they met the problem by describing the "suspension of disbelief" as similar to the mindset we develop when watching a movie or seeing a play. The next day, when students entered the class, they understood they were now in the role of state legislators through a signal the teacher gave indicating the beginning of their problem experience. Throughout the problem experience, he also used props, such as realistic briefing packets that included the state seal and name placards for each representative.

Managing Group Work. Another important part of the PBL process for coaches is managing student group work. Group work can help promote creative problem solving and higher-order thinking skills as well as develop an appreciation of diversity and teamwork (Cohen 1994). Cooperative group work has also been linked with higher performance on complex, ill-structured problems (Qin, Johnson, and Johnson 1995). Some students enter PBL with a good deal of group work experiences (positive or negative); others, with none. Yet because the typical expectation in PBL is that students will work in groups both for information gathering and sharing and for presenting their

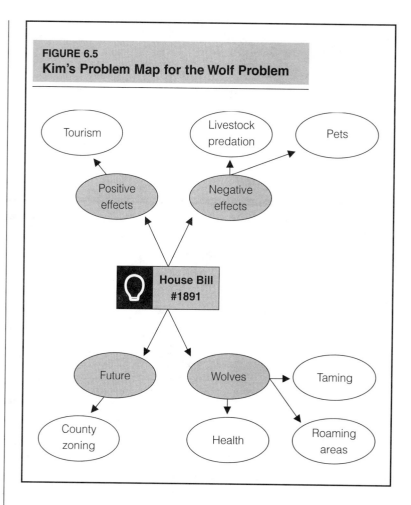

FIGURE 6.5
Kim's Problem Map for the Wolf Problem

solutions, effective preparation for, and management of, group work are essential. PBL coaches, particularly with students inexperienced in group work, may need to prepare students in some areas. Here are examples:

FIGURE 6.6
Kim's Problem Map for the Wolf Problem

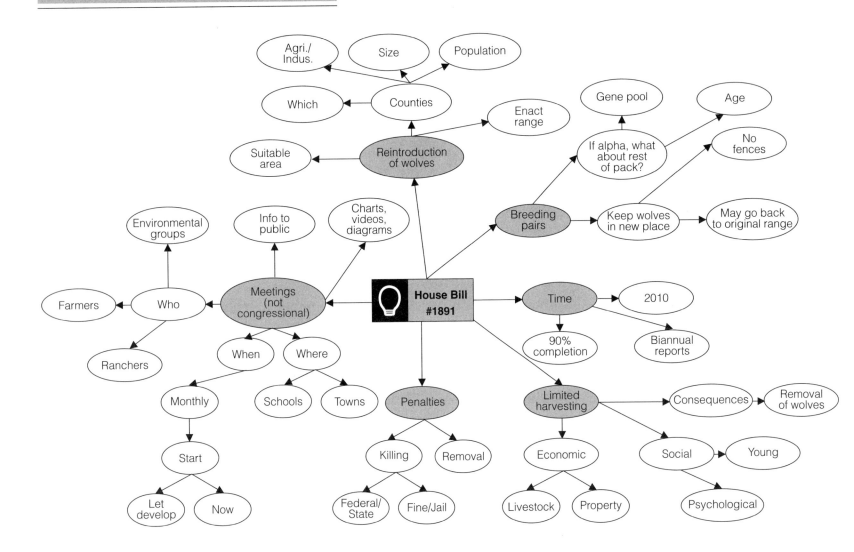

- Listening.
- Reflecting on what has been said.
- Allowing everyone to contribute.
- Sharing information with all members of the group.
- Pulling ideas together.
- Finding out if the group is ready to make a decision.
- Ensuring individual and group accountability.

Elizabeth Cohen's book, *Designing Groupwork* (1994), has some excellent suggestions for activities PBL coaches might use to prepare students for group work or to assist with group problems that arise during a PBL experience.

Two particular areas of challenge in group work are in the sharing of information and in assessment. One strategy PBL coaches often use for information gathering is for a small group of students to work on particular "need-to-know" questions the class has identified. How can the information that the group gathers best be shared with the entire class? The jigsaw method works well: Experts on particular questions are divided among groups so that each group has one expert for presenting solutions in each important area. Other coaches, particularly those with younger students, may choose to have expert groups present information through visual or oral class presentations. Coaches must also manage information gathering and sharing so that they last as long as necessary for the complexity and nature of the problem, but not so long that students become bored or find repetitive information.

Assessments for group work must include both individual and group accountability. Some coaches accomplish this goal by structuring individual assessments while students are working on the problem, such as journals or logs, and planning the presentation of solutions as group accountability. Coaches often develop rubrics with their students for scoring culminating performances, such as oral presentations, displays, and videos. Rubrics help members of the presentation groups not only take more ownership in the overall quality of the presentation, but also be aware of which indicators of quality they will be assessed on.

Monitoring Student Engagement. Finally, throughout the PBL process, coaches must monitor the engagement of students and intervene with nonparticipating students when necessary. Thompson identified several students who often physically isolated themselves from the rest of the class and who were not contributing substantively to gathering information. A large part of his class time in PBL was whole class discussion, which was used for small groups to share the information they had gathered. He instituted the use of "talking chips" (Kagan 1989): Students had to contribute to the discussion enough times to use up their chips, but could not contribute when their chips were gone. This strategy also works well with students who tend to dominate group discussions. Coaches may also, through probing questions, need to identify why particular students have chosen to disengage themselves from the problem, and perhaps encourage them to pursue an area of inquiry that is personally motivating.

Embedding Instruction and Assessment

> The primary purpose of classroom assessment is to inform teaching and improve learning. This premise suggests assessment be viewed as an ongoing process instead of a single event at the conclusion of instruction. . . . Assessment for learning recognizes the mutually supportive relationship between instruction and assessment. Like a mobius strip where one side appears to seamlessly blend into the other, classroom assessment should reflect and promote good instruction.
>
> —McTighe 1996

The glue that holds together all the coaching strategies presented in this chapter is an understanding of the relationship among curriculum, instruction, and assessment. Ongoing assessments throughout the problem experience help coaches determine students' learning needs and then embed instruction in various authentic ways.

Embedded instruction refers to instructional events planned by the PBL teacher to help students explore important information related to the problem. These events may be planned during the design of the problem or during the course of the problem, as students identify a need for knowing certain information. For example, often the best information about a problem resides with people. Teachers may plan to invite local experts on a particular issue as guest speakers or mentors for students. Typically, this type of instructional event looks like a question-and-answer session, in which students may ask their own "need-to-know" questions, rather than listen to an expert's presentation.

Sometimes teachers we encounter initially think that incorporating lessons on particular content or skills is not allowed in PBL or other constructivist strategies. On the contrary! The problematic situation often provides a perfect context for students to have a need for knowing certain information, and embeds the learning in an authentic context. For example, Thompson had identified hunting as a critical predator issue in designing the wolf problem. When students in late stages of information gathering had not yet emphasized this crucial aspect of the proposed legislation, he inserted an authentic lesson on hunting (the kill site demonstration mentioned earlier in the chapter). He embedded this lesson authentically in the problem by asking a colleague to role-play an irate hunter who contacted several students by telephone to ask them to examine the kill site on their school property. Thompson also embedded instructional events by planning field trips to observe wolves at a local zoo and a regional wolf park. Coaches may plan to work with small groups on such needed skills as letter writing or mathematical computation as students encounter a need to know such knowledge for locating information or solving the problem.

Embedded assessments provide teachers with a sense of students' thinking at various points in the sequence of the problem. They also prompt students to address relationships among important events and learning during the problem experience. Such ongoing assessments may take a variety of forms to fit the learner and the problem experience (see Figure 6.7). Based on assessment results, coaches may redirect the problem through instructional events or work with particular students to aid their understanding of the whole and parts of the problem.

FIGURE 6.7
Assessment Possibilities in PBL

PBL Event	Products	Forms	Criteria
Problem Clarification and Identification *Teacher Role:* Read and listen to students present individual problem statements.	Problem statement	Journal entry Problem map Oral presentation Poster Abstract Statement displays	Considers: Nature of problem Problem complexity Operativeness Solvability
Plan Development *Teacher Role:* Review tasks and listen to students clarify plans.	Plan	Task analysis Time line Gantt chart Flow chart Steps Proposal Budget	Uses tasks that control extraneous variables and are Comprehensive Logical Clear Related to nature of problem
Data Collection and Inference Testing *Teacher Role:* Observe, review notes and data, and read journals.	Data records Use of tools Practice of skills	Tables Charts Field notes Microscope use Instrumentation Interviews Observations Quizzes using notes	Records data accurately. Uses tools correctly. Practices skills precisely.
Data Analysis *Teacher Role:* Read and analyze tables, graphs, distribution, etc.	Summary of findings Frequency tables and statistical tables	Summary statements with supporting data Compiled evidence	Uses correct statistical techniques. Makes logical interpretations. Shares collaboratively.
Synthesizing Capstone Performance *Teacher Role:* Observe and assess performance.	Exhibition and recital	News article Poem Decision Recommendation Argument Speech Debate	Displays inventiveness. Relates solution or decision to problem definition. Incorporates problem parameters in solution.

Source: Adapted from Musial 1996.

Thompson used two forms of embedded assessment in the wolf problem: problem maps (see Figures 6.5 and 6.6) and thinking logs. He could look at each map and determine where student learning needs were at that time. He could choose to have students map their understanding of the problem several times, and use the evolving maps and comparisons with an expert map as forms of assessment. Thompson also read and responded to student log entries periodically throughout the problem to assess their progress and diagnose their learning needs.

Summary

In this chapter on implementing PBL, we discussed the teacher's role as coach and the students' role as active learners. We discussed why, how, and what we coach. Finally, we discussed in depth the PBL coach's main responsibilities, including facilitating student understanding, managing the PBL process, and embedding instruction and assessment throughout the sequence of the problem.

In the final chapter, we anticipate your questions as you consider PBL as a curriculum and instructional strategy in your classroom.

7

WHY PROBLEM-BASED LEARNING?

THIS CHAPTER GETS AT THE CENTRAL QUESTION, WHY PBL? The question begs different answers dependent upon one's perspective or role. We are always challenged to think beyond the surface question and address the deeper concerns of the questioner—whether teacher, student, principal, curriculum coordinator, parent, or school business partner. In this chapter, we address these deeper concerns by offering answers to questions educators ask about PBL.

Why change?

John Abbott (1996) makes a strong argument for what he calls the "new competencies"—skills that go far beyond the 19th century basics taught in many schools. The "old competencies" of numeracy, literacy, calculation, and communication are still necessary to begin to function in modern society, but they are not enough. For success in our ever-changing world, the ability to conceptualize problems and solutions is essential. Abbott asserts that the new competencies that must be nurtured and developed include the following:

- **Abstraction.** The mental manipulation of thoughts and patterns in a purposive and ongoing manner.
- **Systems thinking.** The ability to see the interrelatedness of things and the effect of parts upon the whole and the whole upon parts.
- **Experimentation.** The questioning frame of mind that encourages hypothesizing, testing, and evaluating data.
- **Collaboration.** The disposition to be open-minded and adaptable as we coconstruct knowledge together.

These competencies parallel the call for workplace know-how highlighted by the Secretary's Commission for Achieving Necessary Skills (SCANS) (U.S. Department of Labor 1991). Built on a foundation of basic skills, thinking skills, and personal qualities, the SCANS competencies include the following:

- **Resources.** Allocating time, money, and materials.
- **Interpersonal skills.** Working on teams, leading others, negotiating, and showing tolerance.
- **Information.** Acquiring, organizing, evaluating, and interpreting data.
- **Systems.** Understanding social, organizational, and technological systems.

- **Technology.** Selecting and applying technology appropriately.

What makes problem-based learning an attractive strategy for preparing our students for the future?

PBL classrooms are learning communities where information and the construction of knowledge are collective activities. Once information is gathered, shared, and added to the knowledge pool, it is assessed for validity and integrated as appropriate. Expertise grows among community members through dialogue, jigsaw, questioning, reciprocal teaching, and mentoring. Individual learners must then synthesize this knowledge into a holistic understanding of the problem at hand.

Hewitt and Scardamalia's (1996) development of the knowledge-building community model supports our work with problem-based learning communities. They have identified the following characteristics of such communities:

- Inquiry is focused upon communal problems of understanding where meaning is negotiated through questioning, theory refinement, and dialogue.
- Students' ideas about what they need to know become the focus of inquiry.
- Knowledge is shared and held collectively. New information that is shared has the potential of shaping subsequent investigations by others.

- The artifacts of student inquiry are made public and used in knowledge production. These include problem maps that integrate information and highlight connections, graphic organizers that help visualize patterns and relationships, and loop writing that provides opportunities for students to respond to the thinking of their peers.
- Responsibility for planning, organizing, questioning, and summarizing is shared among the students and facilitated by the teacher.

The challenge of higher education in the face of an information explosion, as well as the demands of the high-performance workplace, has clearly established a need to prepare our students for an increasingly complex environment. Problem solving and the higher-order thinking skills of analysis, synthesis, and evaluation are not learned through direct instruction. They emerge from the direct experience of doing. PBL provides that experience.

How do you know that PBL works?

PBL has a rich history in professional schools (medical, dental, nursing, engineering, and business) going back decades. Research conducted to assess the effectiveness of PBL programs cites certain benefits, including increased motivation, sustained self-directed learning behaviors, long-term knowledge retention, comparable content coverage with traditional approaches, learning for understand-ing, and the development of professional reasoning strategies (Albanese and Mitchell 1993, Hendley 1996, Vernon and Blake 1993). Although interesting, this research is not what K–12 teachers, principals, and parents want to know. Their bottom-line question, "Will it work for *my* students?" is one that they must answer for themselves.

PBL has been used at the K–12 levels for several years. Anecdotal evidence is highly supportive. Teachers consistently report increased student engagement in the learning process, increased student responsibility for learning, and deeper levels of understanding. Library and media specialists report that students use more library materials, develop effective search strategies, and gain in information literacy. Principals report that discipline referrals and absenteeism decrease. Parents report hearing about what is happening at school *without having to ask.*

If I use PBL with my students, what will happen to their learning or achievement?

Teachers and principals repeatedly raise this important question. In today's educational climate, one key concern is *to do no harm.* Two middle grade teachers, Karoline Krynock and Louise Robb (1996), investigated the question, Can students gain the same or greater depth and breadth of knowledge through a problem-based unit as through a standard unit?

In a rigorous study, they compared four sections of science classes—two standard, two PBL—on content achievement in a genetics unit in the 8th grade curriculum. Teaching strategies and the curriculum organization differed, but the content was identical. A common instrument was used and scored to assess content achievement or attainment. These results were compared against district-administered standardized test scores aggregated by class. All four classes were directly comparable on this standardized measure of intellectual ability, but the *PBL classes scored slightly higher on the genetics content assessment.* Krynock and Robb go on to say:

> One of the concerns with conducting this kind of research is that the problem-based unit, by nature, covers much more than just the genetics material. Therefore, we not only looked at raw test scores, but also considered the additional skills and habits of mind the students in the PBL class gained from the experience to determine how much material was covered (Krynock and Robb 1996, pp. 22–23).

The PBL classes were also expected to research a messy, ill-structured problem and provide evidence to support their conclusions. They had to write a persuasive position paper and present their conclusions before a panel of professionals knowledgeable in the field of behavioral genetics. During the problem debriefing, students went beyond the testable material and reported that they learned how to do the following:

- Investigate a complex issue.
- Collaborate with peers as learning colleagues in groups.
- Look beyond print material for information and contact experts directly.
- Present their information to a panel of experts.
- Take a position and defend their conclusions using data.
- Think about multiple solutions instead of jumping to conclusions.

Although this study was well done and is highly regarded (winner of a state-level research award), what's important here goes beyond the study results. These educators are not only able to describe their program clearly to parents, students, and administrators, but also to answer the deeper questions of What works? and How do we know?

If PBL does no harm, what is its value-added nature?

Comments from educators describe benefits outside PBL:

- Sue Raben, a learning center director, tells about the experiences of three 3rd grade classes as they investigated issues surrounding zoos, the animals the zoos shelter, and the people who visit the animals. The experiences followed the incident involving Bhinti, the gorilla, and the little boy she rescued at the Brookfield Zoo outside Chicago in 1996.

The children generated ideas and questions and then classified their statements and questions into four categories: natural habitat, zoo habitat, natural behavior, and zoo behavior. They investigated these issues in small groups. The excitement that PBL generated was almost overwhelming. Children did not want to stop.

Raben reports that the students felt empowered—certainly not limited—by their own reading and writing abilities. Parents whose children were involved were equally excited. One parent of a child with serious learning disabilities commented that this was the first time her child came home eager to talk about a project.

- Richard Dods (1996), a science/chemistry teacher, writes:

> Although process is emphasized [in PBL], content is not lost. Ongoing action research studies [in his course] compare students who have experienced PBL biochemistry with those who have experienced biochemistry in an interactive questioning format. Results suggest that the PBL biochemistry approach promotes deeper understanding of biochemical content and longer-term recall of content than the interactive questioning format (p. 228).

Dods believes that a student's "problem-based frame of mind" provides a web of understanding that meaningfully connects individual pieces of content. These connections enable access and recall through multiple avenues that support deeper levels of understanding.

- Ellen Jo Ljung, a language arts teacher, has designed a PBL Communications and Technology (Comm-Tech)

course for sophomores, juniors, and seniors. She is presently engaged in a yearlong action research study to assess the effectiveness of this class in developing students' skills in critical thinking and communication, as well as to identify "essential qualities" of a Glenbard West High School graduate. Ljung is gathering data in many areas; one is student perceptions. She used a Venn diagram to elicit student feedback, then combined the results from individual students (see Figure 7.1 on p. 84).

Ljung's Comm-Tech students have identified and investigated several actual community problems. One group focused on the need for a teen club within the village of Glendale Heights, Illinois. Three students presented their ideas before the village trustees (Mawhorr 1996). The trustees agreed to consider the proposal (Pohl 1996), which included the following elements:

- The club would be open Friday and Saturday nights, with a cover charge of $7.00.
- Students 17 and younger would leave by 11:00 p.m. because of the village curfew.
- Only water and soft drinks would be served, and a dress code would be enforced.
- Metal detectors would be used at the entrance, and security guards would circulate.

Another Comm-Tech student group "sought to raise awareness and eliminate misconceptions about homelessness in Glen Ellyn," Illinois (Pohl 1997). They surveyed 100 business owners and employees in the downtown area and found that 54 percent identified a homeless problem and 20 percent thought that it affected business. Students then prepared a brochure to share the survey results, provide information about what businesses and citizens could do to help, and explain resources and services available to assist homeless people. These students certainly got below the surface of the issue and demonstrated deeper levels of understanding.

If a PBL approach empowers students to "deeper levels of understanding," what contributes to that outcome?

"Teaching for understanding" is a phrase heard frequently today in education, but student understanding is an elusive thing to define—let alone capture. Rebecca Simmons (1994), project manager for the Teaching for Understanding Project at Harvard, describes understanding in this way:

> We want students to be able to employ knowledge in flexible and novel ways, to develop flexible networks of concepts, to use what they learn in school to understand the world around them, and to develop interest in lifelong intellectual pursuits. But to help students achieve such understanding is no mean feat (p. 22).

PBL employs several features that many believe move students toward deeper levels of understanding—such as embedded assessment and role playing.

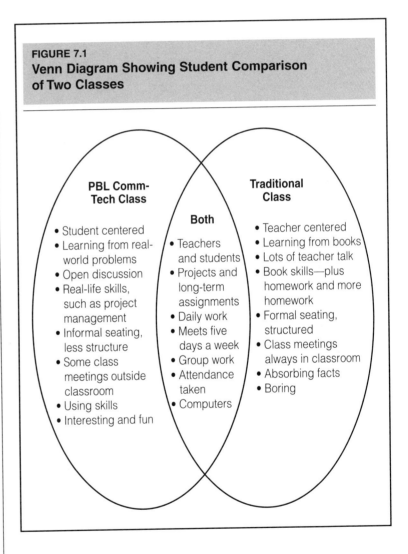

FIGURE 7.1

Venn Diagram Showing Student Comparison of Two Classes

PBL Comm-Tech Class
- Student centered
- Learning from real-world problems
- Open discussion
- Real-life skills, such as project management
- Informal seating, less structure
- Some class meetings outside classroom
- Using skills
- Interesting and fun

Both
- Teachers and students
- Projects and long-term assignments
- Daily work
- Meets five days a week
- Group work
- Attendance taken
- Computers

Traditional Class
- Teacher centered
- Learning from books
- Lots of teacher talk
- Book skills—plus homework and more homework
- Formal seating, structured
- Class meetings always in classroom
- Absorbing facts
- Boring

Embedded Assessment

This kind of ongoing assessment *for learning* places students within a dynamic framework of assessment events that are driven by four factors:

- **Expectation.** Students know that the products of their learning—such as journals, logs, letters, diagrams, predictions, position papers, presentations, progress reports, and problem statements—are substantiated with evidence and reflect benchmarks of good thinking (Perkins 1992). This type of learning moves students to appreciate evidence over assertion and learning over replication.
- **Performance.** Student performances or products, whether written or oral, representational or dramatic, place them in the problem's center as knowledge producers. These products must be "thought-demanding" (Perkins 1993b, p. 7). Stretching students beyond what they comfortably know helps them recognize the tentative nature of what is known at any point in time and how this tentativeness may affect the problem, further investigation, and possible solutions. Performance resides in this problem space, where "both person and environment change over the course of the transaction" (Bredo 1996, p. 3).
- **Feedback.** To progress, students must test their understanding against the thinking of others and evaluate the feedback. These others include peers, teachers, experts, parents, and community members. Feedback also makes learning a process characterized by rethinking, refining, restating, representing, renovating, and reconstructing.

- **Integration and Elaboration.** New understanding from further investigation, from the products of peers, from feedback, and from thought and reflection needs to be integrated into a holistic understanding and then stretched to see how it connects to the bigger picture and has meaning for students' lives. Assessment then becomes a series of ongoing learning events fueling the learning process, rather than endpoints signaling closure (Simmons 1994).

Beyond Role Playing

Role playing pushes students beyond learning facts and discrete skills into the middle of the problem, where they must make sense of its reality. Embracing the role of a stakeholder dramatically increases students' ownership of the situation. They more easily recognize varying perspectives on the situation and the conflicting conditions placed upon any solution. Both the thinking and feeling aspects of the problem come into focus, providing a vehicle for deeper levels of understanding.

Fred Newmann of the University of Wisconsin has extensively investigated higher-order thinking skills in the social sciences. Newmann's findings indicate that both cognition and affect are inseparable. His model (Newmann 1990) proposes that students move from empathy to abstraction to inference to evaluation to advocacy. Role playing enables students to make that empathic connection to the problem and facilitates their journey toward advocacy and taking a public stand on the issue.

Diann Musial and Liz Hammerman (1997) of Northern Illinois University describe the intimate perspective of PBL learners:

> The problem-based learner tends to develop mental patterns that are highly connected to the richness of the problem situation. Such understanding is highly integrated and linked to a variety of real-world situations, perspectives, disciplines, etc. Such learners are able to answer essay questions not only in terms of the definition of terms; they are able to elaborate on the meaning of important ideas and add nuances that are connected to the real world. This is so, *not* because they have read about those connections, but because they have experienced the connections first hand (p. 6) (emphasis in original).

What are the barriers that thwart PBL adoption?

We find that most educators with whom we work recognize the importance of PBL to increase student motivation to deeper levels of understanding. Yet the mantra of coverage still dominates in many areas, often because our major evaluation instruments drive what gets taught. Many teachers are faced with restrictive schedules or other structures that work against the time necessary for student engagement and teaching for understanding. They also express frustration with a lack of time during the school day for designing new problems.

Still other teachers are fearful of change because they are constrained by school norms that perpetuate the status quo. Some teachers feel they are "out on a limb" using PBL in their classes. As one middle school teacher reported overhearing another teacher say: "Where are the worksheets? Where are the tests? . . . They [students] are laughing, they're having fun, they're running around wanting to do research; what is this?"

Teachers and teaching teams who recognize any or all of these obstacles within their schools work proactively to build and nurture support among colleagues and community. Many have enlisted parents as both allies and resources for PBL units. Others tap the knowledge and expertise of school colleagues to serve as mentors in problem inquiries. Although innovation and change can ignite fears and create barriers, communication and openness can reveal unseen possibilities.

The interplay between enabling structures and sustaining commitments is a ballet of give and take while an innovation is taking hold. Another essential component is support from administrators—support for PBL as well as support provided through resources and assistance with accessing appropriate information. We find most principals eager to support innovations that enhance student learning.

What does it take to become a teacher of PBL?

We have found that PBL requires a facility to use a coaching style that preservice and inservice experiences often do not address. As an ongoing part of our professional development activities, we asked teachers to reflect on what they were learning about teaching PBL (Sage and Torp 1997) and concluded the following:

• **Making the transition from teacher as information-giver to teacher as coach is challenging and requires learning new skills.** Teachers discussed giving up the idea that they had to be the expert. Some found it difficult to let go of the sense of control and predictability typical in more traditional instruction; but eventually most teachers came to realize that, as Mary Biddle put it, "Not only do I need to let go, I need to stay there [to provide support to students]." Teachers also learned in their role as coach how to question students' thinking and to challenge students to support their conclusions. Laurie Friedrich, a staff development coordinator, said, "We learned that we needed to focus our language on the language of *thinking.*"

• **Designing problem scenarios requires a sound understanding of problem-based learning, curriculum, and authentic assessment.** Teachers wrestled with the design of problem scenarios as they worked to integrate required curriculum outcomes and incorporate the teaching and assessment of meaningful skills throughout the problem. Considering *what* content their problems would address also challenged teachers to consider essential knowledge of disciplines rather than automatically using content as defined by textbooks. As teachers designed assessments, they had to consider how to use them so that the assessment measured student thinking and guided, but did not limit, learning. Teachers also found they were teaching skills, such as writing business letters, in more authentic ways—that is, teaching in the context of the problem rather than in isolation.

• **Learning in a PBL environment is exciting for students and rewarding for teachers.** Teachers found that seeing what students could do led them to *trust* their students more. Lisa Nicholson, a special education instructor, said, "PBL has proven to me that if you don't give the kids limitations and if you overlook their disabilities, PBL gives them the chance to learn the way they need to learn." Teachers believed that because PBL encourages students to explore information in different ways—such as through print, telephone, and the Internet—and to learn about authentic problems, it was also a motivating strategy for students with varied learning styles and strengths.

We have discovered that teachers of PBL benefit from multiple supports, including active support in their buildings from administrators and other teachers. Team teaching has been an effective method of support. If other teachers in the building are not implementing PBL, then teachers need a network of other practitioners with whom to share ideas and get help. We have established such a network for our teachers as well as an electronic mail list (see Appendix). This networking is particularly critical for more experienced PBL practitioners to communicate with others who have similar concerns (Gibbons 1995).

We have found, too, that often teachers don't fully "buy in" to PBL, particularly to their role as coaches, until they've tried it and seen how powerful the experience is for their students. It is also particularly helpful for teachers to see as many examples as possible of PBL problems other teachers at their level have designed and implemented. That is one reason we used so many examples in this book. In addition, we have found that *using* PBL to *teach* PBL is essential, so that teachers experience PBL as learners first (Sage and Torp 1997). Like any effective learning experience for students, teachers also benefit from a collaborative climate of learning challenges and appropriate support (see Figure 7.2).

In Closing

For PBL practitioners, there is no question about the effectiveness of PBL. These educators point to many positive effects:

- Students who were turned off by more traditional approaches emerging as active, engaged learners.
- Students who can talk about a topic in depth—not simply answer factual questions.
- Students who *ask* for targeted lessons about what they need to know to solve a problem.

- Students who ask good questions that reflect an understanding deeper than any response shows.
- Students who know how to locate, evaluate, and use information effectively.
- And, of course, students who learn and perform well on content tests.

Problem-based learning has been used in urban and rural settings, with elementary and secondary students, reluctant learners, and eager learners—in short, with students of all abilities and ages in almost every subject area. PBL consistently gets high marks from students, parents, and administrators whenever the teacher is motivated and well versed in PBL techniques. PBL exposes solid, demanding content; engages students at an emotional level; and fosters skills needed in a complex world. It is a curriculum organizer and instructional strategy that can be implemented whenever learning goals demand deeper understandings—whether occasionally or frequently—in tandem with other strategies. We believe PBL is a powerful technique that all teachers should have in their repertoire for the 21st century.

FIGURE 7.2
Balancing Professional Development Challenges with Needed Support

Fundamental Questions That Drive PBL Professional Development

- What is my role as teacher in PBL?
- What new skills do I need?
- How should we prepare students as citizens in tomorrow's world?

- What knowledge is most critical?
- How do we assess student learning in PBL?
- How do we communicate effectively about PBL to others?

DIMENSION	CHALLENGES	SUPPORT
Context	• Philosophical differences within the school community • Isolation from professional peers • Questionable level of administrative support • Parent and community relations	• Appropriate resources • Teaming with colleagues • Active administrative backing • Electronic network to facilitate dialogue across sites and professional contexts
Teaching	• Integrating complex understandings • Adopting new practices • Assuming a new role • Modifying grounding beliefs • Modulating concerns	• Appropriate information when needed • Collegial dialogue • Modeling by experienced coaches • Practice in a safe environment • Mentoring by PBL practitioners
Learning	• Creating authentic learning situations • Integrating content and process • Coaching and managing active student learning • Capturing the effects of PBL teaching and learning	• Coaching student learning • Practice and mentoring • Evidence of student learning and growth • Collegial network of PBL practitioners

Appendix:

How Can I Learn More About
Problem-Based Learning?

I. ASCD Member Network

The Problem-Based Learning Network (PBL Net) is one of ASCD's member networks. Our goal is to create a strong base of support for problem-based learning among educators at all levels. Problem-based learning enhances understanding through more relevant, connected learning and taps students' natural curiosity about the world around them to ignite motivation for

Appendix: How Can I Learn More About Problem-Based Learning?

91

learning. Students are engaged in learning about issues that challenge them to apply what they have learned in authentic ways.

PBL Net maintains and supports an interpersonal and electronic network to enable dialogue and the sharing of information, methods, and materials. We strive to enhance our understanding of problem-based learning from the perspectives of *learner*, *coach*, and *problem designer*.

Our award-winning newsletter, *The Problem Log*, connects and inspires our members. Articles are submitted by acknowledged experts in PBL, as well as practitioners eager to share classroom experiences. Reflections of teachers in the midst of changing teaching and learning in their classrooms, reports of teachers' action research related to PBL, and dissemination of relevant research about PBL (K–16) round out each issue.

Member fees are $15.00 per year and are due on the anniversary of initial membership. Members receive three issues of *The Problem Log* each year. PBL Net holds an annual meeting and discussion forum scheduled concurrently with the ASCD Annual Conference.

For membership information contact: Center for Problem-Based Learning, Illinois Mathematics and Science Academy, 1500 W. Sullivan Road, Aurora, Illinois 60506 USA; or e-mail: pbl-info@imsa.edu; or call 630-907-5956 or 630-907-5957.

II. Listserv

An Internet Listserv (IMSACPBL-L) facilitates online dialogue among those interested and working in problem-based learning. This list is maintained at the Illinois Mathematics and Science Academy and is made possible through additional funding provided by The Hitachi Foundation.

To subscribe:

Send mail to: MAJORDOMO@IMSA.EDU

With the message: subscribe imsacpbl-l [your e-mail address]

To send mail:

Send mail to: IMSACPBL-L@IMSA.EDU

To get more information about using the list:

Send mail to: MAJORDOMO@IMSA.EDU

With the message: HELP

III. Threaded Discussion Forum

We also moderate a threaded discussion forum on ASCD's WWW site: <http://www.ascd.org/>. Click on Communication & Forums; then click on ASCD Network: Problem-Based Learning. Add your thoughts and comments to the ongoing discussion.

IV. World Wide Web Site

The WWW address is <http://www.imsa.edu/team/ cpbl/>. This site provides information related to the following key questions:

- What is the Center for Problem-Based Learning?
- What is problem-based learning (PBL)?
- What does PBL look like in a K–12 classroom?
- Who is doing PBL?
- Who can I contact to learn more?

The site includes other information:

- The Bison Commons. Interactive WWW-based PBL problem for middle grade and high school students, complete with problem information links and a Teacher Information Center.
- SUPERLAND! A WWW-based PBL problem used in the Summer AD'Ventures program for middle grade students, complete with individual student products.

V. The Illinois Mathematics and Science Academy's Center for PBL

The Illinois Mathematics and Science Academy (IMSA) is an educational laboratory for designing and testing innovative programs and methods to share with other teachers and schools in Illinois and beyond. Included in the laboratory is a three-year (grades 10–12) residential program for Illinois students talented in mathematics and science.

The Academy's mission is "to transform mathematics and science teaching and learning by developing ethical leaders who know the joy of discovering and forging connections within and among mathematics, science, the arts, and the humanities by means of an exemplary laboratory environment characterized by innovative teaching, research, and service."

To advance IMSA's mission, the Academy established the Center for Problem-Based Learning in 1992. The Center for Problem-Based Learning engages in PBL professional development, curriculum development, research, information exchange, and networking in K–16 educational settings. The Center for Problem-Based Learning has three goals:

- To mentor educators in all disciplines as they design and develop effective problem-based learning materials and become skillful coaches.
- To explore problem-based learning strategies as the context in which knowledge is acquired, ethical decision making is nurtured, and problem-solving skills are developed.
- To connect problem-based learning educators through numerous networking options designed to meet a variety of needs.

REFERENCES

Abbott, J. (1996). "A New Synthesis for Effective Learning." *Wingspread Journal* 17, 2: 10–12.

Albanese, M.A., and S. Mitchell. (1993). "Problem-Based Learning: A Review of Literature on Its Outcomes and Implementation Issues." *Academic Medicine* 68, 1: 52–81.

Alkove, L., and B. McCarthy. (1992). "Plain Talk: Recognizing Positivism and Constructivism in Practice." *Action in Teacher Education* 14, 2: 9–15.

American Association for the Advancement of Science, Project 2061. (1993). *Benchmarks for Science Literacy.* New York: Oxford University Press.

Aspy, D.N., C.B. Aspy, and P.M. Quinby. (April 1993). "What Doctors Can Teach Teachers About Problem-Based Learning." *Educational Leadership* 50, 7: 22–24.

Barell, J. (1995). "Problem-Based Learning and Crew Members of the *Santa Maria*." In *Teaching for Thoughtfulness*, edited by J. Barell. White Plains, N.Y.: Longman.

Barrows, H., and R. Tamblyn. (1976). "An Evaluation of Problem-Based Learning in Small Groups Using a Simulated Patient." *Journal of Medical Education* 51, 1: 52–54.

Barrows, H.S. (1988). *The Tutorial Process*. Springfield, Ill.: Southern Illinois University School of Medicine.

Benoit, B. (Spring 1996). "PBL and the Summer Youth Jobs Program." *The Problem Log* 1, 1: 4.

Bodner, G. (1986). "Constructivism: A Theory of Knowledge." *Journal of Chemical Education* 63, 10: 873–877.

Boix-Mansilla, V., and H. Gardner. (1997). "Of Kinds of Disciplines and Kinds of Understanding." *Phi Delta Kappan* 78, 5: 381–386.

Boud, D., and G. Feletti. (1991). *The Challenge of Problem-Based Learning*. New York: St. Martin's Press.

Bransford, J.D. (April 1993). "Who Ya Gonna Call? Thoughts About Teaching Problem Solving." Paper presented at the annual meeting of the American Educational Research Association, Atlanta.

Bredo, E. (1996). "Cognitivism, Situated Cognition, and Deweyian Pragmatism." <http://www.ed.uiuc.edu/COE/EPS/PESYearbook/94_docs/BREDO.HTM>

Brooks, J.G., and M.G. Brooks. (1993). *In Search of Understanding: The Case for Constructivist Classrooms*. Alexandria, Va.: Association for Supervision and Curriculum Development.

Broudy, H. (May 1982). "What Knowledge Is of Most Worth?" *Educational Leadership* 39, 8: 574–578.

Casey, M., and E. Tucker. (1994). "Problem-Centered Classrooms." *Phi Delta Kappan* 10, 94: 139–143.

Center for Problem-Based Learning. (1996a). *Professional Development Resource Materials*. Aurora, Ill.: Illinois Mathematics and Science Academy.

Center for Problem-Based Learning. (1996b). "Role Playing in Problem-Based Learning." <http://www.imsa.edu/team/cpbl/instruct/Bisonproj/roleplng.html>

Center for Problem-Based Learning. (1996c). "Why Do Mosquitoes Buzz in People's Ears?" Developed for the Harris Institute. Aurora, Ill.: Illinois Mathematics and Science Academy.

Clark, C.M. (1988). "Asking the Right Questions About Teacher Preparation: Contributions of Research on Teacher Thinking." *Educational Researcher* 17, 2: 5–12.

Clarke, J. (1997). "Solving Problems." In *Interdisciplinary High School Teaching*, edited by J. Clarke and R.M. Agne. Boston: Allyn and Bacon.

Cohen, E.G. (1994). *Designing Groupwork: Strategies for the Heterogeneous Classroom*. 2nd ed. New York: Teachers College Press.

Cornbleth, C. (1988). "Curriculum in and out of Context." *Journal of Curriculum and Supervision* 3, 2: 85–96.

Dewey, J. (1916). *Democracy and Education: An Introduction to the Philosophy of Education*. New York: Macmillan.

Dewey, J. (1943). *The School and Society*. Chicago: University of Chicago Press.

Dewey, J. (1991). *How We Think*. Buffalo, N.Y.: Prometheus Books. (Original work published in 1910).

Dods, R. (1996). "A Problem-Based Learning Design for Teaching Biochemistry." *Journal of Chemical Education* 73: 225–228.

Doll, W. (1993). "Curriculum Possibilities in a 'Post'-Future." *Journal of Curriculum and Supervision* 8, 4: 277–292.

Duffy, T.M., and J.R. Savery. (February 1995). "Constructivism: A Theory of Learning with Implications for Instruction." Session presented at the annual meeting of the Association for Educational Communications and Technology, Anaheim, Calif.

Finkle, S., R. Briggs, L. Hinton, J. Thompson, and R. Dods. (1994). "The Summer Challenge Landfill Problem." Aurora, Ill.: Illinois Mathematics and Science Academy.

Gallagher, S., H. Rosenthal, and W. Stepien. (1992). "The Effects of

Problem-Based Learning on Problem-Solving." *Gifted Child Quarterly* 36, 4: 195–200.

Gibbons, D. (1995). "PBL Diffusion: Factors Influencing PBL Knowledge, Teaching Values, and Level of Use." Unpublished report available from the Illinois Mathematics and Science Academy, Aurora, Ill.

Glickman, C. (May 1991). "Pretending Not to Know What We Know." *Educational Leadership* 48, 8: 4–10.

Greenberg, J. (1990). *Problem-Solving Situations*. Vol. 1. Corvallis, Oreg.: Grapevine Publications, Inc.

Harris, K.R., and S. Graham. (February 1996). "Memo to Constructivists: Skills Count, Too." *Educational Leadership* 53, 5: 26–29.

Heathcote, D. (1983). "Learning, Knowing, and Language in Drama." *Language Arts* 60, 6: 695–701.

Heathcote, D., and P. Herbert. (1980). "A Drama of Learning: Mantle of the Expert." *Theory into Practice* 24, 3: 173–180.

Hendley, V. (October 1996). "Let Problems Drive the Learning." *AESS Prism*, pp. 30–36.

Hewitt, J., and M. Scardamalia. (1996). "Design Principles for the Support of Distributed Processes." <http://twilight.oise.utoronto.ca/abstracts/distributed>

Illinois Problem-Based Learning Network. (1996). "Don't Let the Smoke Get in Your Eyes." The Summer Sleuths Program. Aurora, Ill.: Illinois Mathematics and Science Academy.

Illinois State Board of Education's Center for Scientific Literacy. (1994). "Scientific Literacy Program: Request for Proposals." Springfield, Ill.: Illinois State Board of Education.

Kagan, S. (1989). *Cooperative Learning Resources for Teachers*. 8th ed. Laguna Niguel, Calif.: Resources for Teachers.

Kitchener, K.S. (1983). "Cognition, Metacognition, and Epistemic Cognition: A Three-Level Model of Cognitive Processing." *Human Development* 26, 4: 222–232.

Krynock, K.B., and L. Robb. (Fall 1996). "Is Problem-Based Learning a Problem for Your Curriculum?" *Illinois School Research and Development Journal* 33, 1: 21–24.

Lave, J., and E. Wenger. (1991). *Situated Learning: Legitimate Peripheral Participation*. Cambridge, United Kingdom: Cambridge University Press.

Lederman, L. (1994). "Give a Small Child a Hammer and Soon Everything Needs Hammering." *Simulation and Gaming* 25, 2: 215–221.

Lipman, M. (September 1988). "Critical Thinking—What Can It Be?" *Educational Leadership* 46, 1: 38–43.

Lipman, M. (1991). *Thinking in Education*. New York: Cambridge University Press.

Mawhorr, S. (December 20, 1996). "Glendale Heights Students, Trustees Discuss Dance Club." *Daily Herald*, p. 4.

McTighe, J. (September 1996). "Toward More Thoughtful Assessment: Principles and Practices." Session at Illinois Association for Supervision and Curriculum Development Research Conference, Naperville.

Musial, D. (1996). "Designing Assessments in a Problem-Based Learning Context." *The Problem Log* 1, 2: 4–5.

Musial, D., and L. Hammerman. (1997). "Framing Ways of Knowing in Problem-Based Learning." Unpublished manuscript.

National Research Council. (1996). *National Science Education Standards*. Washington, D.C.: National Academy Press.

Newmann, F. (1990). "Higher-Order Thinking in Social Studies: A Rationale for the Assessment of Classroom Thoughtfulness." *Journal of Curriculum Studies* 22, 1: 41–56.

Norris, S.P. (May 1985). "Synthesis of Research on Critical Thinking." *Educational Leadership* 42, 5: 40–45.

Perkins, D. (1992). *Smart Schools: From Training Memories to Educating Minds*. New York: The Free Press.

Perkins, D. (1993a). "Teaching for Understanding." *American Educator* 17, 3: 8.

Perkins, D. (1993b). "An Apple for Education: Teaching and Learning for Understanding." Presentation at the EdPress Conference, Philadelphia, Pa.

Piaget, J. (1985). *The Equilibration of Cognitive Structures*. Translated by T. Brown and K.J. Thampy. Chicago: University of Chicago Press. (Original work published in 1975).

Pohl, L. (December 30, 1996). "Village May Open Dance Club for Teens." *Chicago Tribune*, p. 3.

Pohl, L. (January 15, 1997). "Class Tackles Tough Issues with Critical Thinking." Glen Ellyn (Ill.) *Daily Herald*, sec. 5, p. 1.

Qin, Z., D.W. Johnson, and R.T. Johnson. (1995). "Cooperative Versus Competitive Efforts and Problem Solving." *Review of Educational Research* 65, 2: 129–143.

Reigeluth, C.M. (1994). "The Imperative for Systemic Change." In *Systemic Change in Education*, edited by C.M. Reigeluth and R.J. Garfinkle. Englewood Cliffs, N.J.: Educational Technology Publications.

Rorty, R. (1991). *Objectivity, Relativism and Truth: Philosophical Papers*. Vol. I. Cambridge: Cambridge University Press.

Sage, S.M., and L.T. Torp. (1997). "What Does It Take to Become a Teacher of Problem-Based Learning?" *Journal of Staff Development* 18, 4: 32–36.

Savery, J.R., and T.M. Duffy. (1995). "Problem-Based Learning: An Instructional Model and Its Constructivist Framework." *Educational Technology* 35, 5: 31–35.

Scardamalia, M., and C. Bereiter. (1991). "Higher Levels of Agency for Children in Knowledge-Building: A Challenge for Design of New Knowledge Media." *The Journal of Learning Sciences* 1, 1: 38–68.

Simmons, R. (February 1994). "The Horse Before the Cart: Assessing for Understanding." *Educational Leadership* 51, 5: 22–23.

Stepien, W., and S. Gallagher. (April 1993). "Problem-Based Learning: As Authentic as It Gets." *Educational Leadership* 50, 7: 25–28.

Swink, D. (1993). "Role Playing Your Way to Learning." *Training and Development* 47, 5: 91–97.

Sylwester, R. (1995). *A Celebration of Neurons: An Educator's Guide to the Human Brain*. Alexandria, Va.: Association for Supervision and Curriculum Development.

Torp, L.T. (1996). *Planning a Problem-Based Learning Adventure*. Naperville, Ill.: Possibilities, Inc.

U.S. Department of Labor. (1991). *What Work Requires of Schools: A SCANS Report for America 2000*. Washington, D.C.: U.S. Government Printing Office.

Vernon, D., and R. Blake. (1993). "Does Problem-Based Learning Work? A Meta-Analysis of Evaluative Research." *Academic Medicine* 7: 550–563.

Vitale-Ortlund, C. (1994). *Harris Institute for Introduction to Problem-Based Learning Design Products*. Aurora, Ill.: Illinois Mathematics and Science Academy.

von Glasersfeld, E. (1989). "Cognition, Construction of Knowledge, and Teaching." *Synthese* 80: 121–140.

von Glasersfeld, E. (April 1993). "Radical Constructivism: Teaching vs.

Training." Paper presented at the annual meeting of the American Educational Research Association, Atlanta, Ga.

Wagner, B. (1988). "Research Currents: Does Classroom Drama Affect the Arts of Language?" *Language Arts* 65, 1: 46–55.

Whole Earth Catalog. (1971). *The Last Whole Earth Catalog.* Menlo Park, Calif.: Portola Institute, Inc.

Wiggins, G., and H. Jacobs. (November 1995). "Toward Student Understanding: Designing Coherent Curriculum, Assessment, and Instruction." Restructuring Your School: Integrated/Thematic

Curriculum and Performance Assessment Conference, National School Conference Institute, St. Louis.

Willems, J. (1981). "Problem-Based Group Teaching: A Cognitive Science Approach to Using Knowledge." *Instructional Science* 10, 1: 5–21.

Witherell, C., and N. Noddings. (1991). *Stories Lives Tell: Narrative and Dialogue in Education.* New York: Teachers College Press.

Wolf, C., L. McIlvain, and M. Stockburger. (1992). "Getting Our Students to Think Through Simulations." *Contemporary Education* 63, 3: 219–220.

INDEX

Page numbers in boldface italic refer to pages
that contain figures.

ABOUT THE AUTHORS

Linda Torp is Director of Research, Evaluation, and Development at the Illinois Mathematics and Science Academy in Aurora, and Network Facilitator for ASCD's member network, PBL Net. She has served as Director for the Center for Problem-Based Learning and worked as a professional developer for several years in the areas of problem-based learning and integrated curriculum. Her work in schools as an educator and consultant spans elementary through graduate levels.

Torp can be reached at the Illinois Mathematics and Science Academy, 1500 West Sullivan Road, Aurora, IL 60506-1000 USA; telephone: 630-907-5071; e-mail: ltorp@imsa.edu.

Sara Sage is Assistant Professor of Secondary Education at Indiana University, South Bend. She has been a special educator and teacher educator, and has conducted several studies in problem-based learning as a research specialist at the Center for Problem-Based Learning. Her interests include professional development for teachers, human development and learning, and constructivist teaching and learning models.

Sage can be reached at the Division of Education, Indiana University South Bend, P.O. Box 7111, South Bend, IN 46634-7111 USA; telephone: 219-237-6504; e-mail: ssage@iusb.edu.

1 8 1999